I'VE
GOT
TIME

PAUL LOOMANS

I'VE GOT TIME

A Zen monk's guide to a calm, focused and meaningful life

WATKINS
Sharing Wisdom
Since 1893

I've Got Time by Paul Loomans

Originally published in 2017 as *Time Surfing*.

This edition published 2024 by Watkins, an imprint of Watkins Media Limited, Shepperton House, Unit 11 89-93, Shepperton Rd, London N1 3DF

enquiries@watkinspublishing.com

A CIP record for this book is available from the British Library

ISBN: 978-1-78678-917-4 (paperback)
ISBN: 978-1-78678-918-1 (ebook)
10 9 8 7 6 5 4 3 2 1

MIX
Paper | Supporting
responsible forestry
FSC® C171272

Typeset by Lapiz
Printed and bound by CPI Group (UK) Ltd, Croydon, CR0 4YY

www.watkinspublishing.com

CONTENTS

Follow the QR code for an introductory video
by the author on Time Surfing

INTRODUCTION

This book is intended to serve as both an inspiration and a guide in choosing calm as the starting point for all your daily activities, whether at work, at home or while travelling. It describes a method that consists of seven instructions, each of which will be set out in the pages that follow.

Above all, this method is enjoyable and user-friendly. It doesn't require any special discipline, and you don't need to constantly monitor yourself while practising it. On the contrary, because its instructions are based on natural human behaviour, the more you use the method, the more natural it feels and the easier it becomes. Those who attend my workshops and classes on "Unravelling Stress" in Amsterdam often tell me how surprised they are that such simple guidelines can have such an effect.

Also, anyone can use this method. I have seen it used successfully by a neurologist, a manager, teachers, students, a gardener, as well as by those looking for work. Some people, such as my doctor's secretary, already use it on their own to a certain extent.

In a nutshell, the method that follows allows you to transition from **control** – the way many of us seek to organize our lives, to **trust** – the foundation for creating a fluid relationship with time.

I call this "Time Surfing": using intuition to navigate over the waves of time.

When you deal with time in this way, in addition to an underlying sense of calm, you will also get satisfaction from whatever you're doing, and naturally be able to give it your undivided attention. What's more, because you feel inspired, your actions will also be effective.

This might sound too good to be true, especially when I tell you that the transition can happen surprisingly quickly.

I invite you to embark on this adventure with confidence, so that you too will soon be able to experience the enjoyable mix of restfulness and dynamism that is Time Surfing.

How this book is structured

That we live in an increasingly fast-paced world is something that's very noticeable these days. There never seems to be enough time in the day. In the first section, I describe what causes this time pressure. You'll discover that although the world around us is certainly one of the factors involved, it's not the only reason – and, in my view, not the most important reason – for feeling stressed when doing the things we need to do. Here I'll also talk about my own experiences with time pressure – experiences that led me to take a radical decision and, in the process, discover the key principles of this method.

For me, this path of discovery was filled with surprises. In the end I felt as if I'd uncovered something that already existed but that was not widely accessible because it hadn't yet been clearly examined and set out. My own stumbling blocks, I hope, can serve as lessons, saving you time and trouble during your own transition. If you're impatient (which you still may be at the moment …) and want to get started immediately, you can jump ahead to Part II, which sets out the seven elements of Time Surfing. To provide you with an overview, these are first described in brief. A detailed discussion of each will then follow.

As you progress through the method, you can immediately start to apply the individual instructions to the way you approach tasks and activities. The change will only be complete, however, when you apply the final instruction: "Use your intuition when choosing what to do." That's the moment you push out from shore and surf through time using trust and intuition as your guide. So don't be tempted to skip ahead – the conditions for this final push out into open water are created by Instructions 1 through 6, so you'll need to master these first.

Once you're using the method in its entirety and you've started to Time Surf, I would recommend that you pick one of the instructions and pay special attention to this over the course of one or more days. In this way, each instruction will become more and more familiar to you, and after a while you'll find yourself using them without having to focus on the method at all because it will become second nature to you.

When you put your trust in this new system – something that's necessary for it to be able to function properly – it's possible to make the transition in a few weeks to a few months.

The book closes with explanations of several applications and tools, each of which requires special attention. First off, we'll examine the phenomenon of "the deadline". After looking at the body reflex it often provokes, you'll be encouraged to approach these in a completely different way.

Another section is devoted to dealing with email. You'll get practical tips that are in keeping with the method and specifically aimed at what has become one of our most important means of communication.

The smartphone and social media have, within the last two decades, elbowed their way into our already busy schedules. Their impact on our daily lives and on Time Surfing is the subject of the third section in this part.

We'll then take a look at your appointment calendar, workplace and lists – specifically, how a Time Surfer will use these tools effectively.

And, finally, there's a section on sense perception. I like to think of this theme as the "icing on the cake". Although you don't need it to be able to use the method, it's a valuable addition and, because it gives flavour and colour to everything you do and experience, may be more essential than you first thought.

From a Zen perspective

Because I practise Zen intensively, the influence of Zen can be felt throughout the method. For me, Zen is like a spring, and the transparent droplets that form this method came bubbling up out of its depths.

It's in a particular way of looking at things that Zen can be found. For example, facing things directly, even the things you find difficult. Or observing something you'd like to change so that the change can happen on its own rather than through force. Trusting your gut feelings and not overvaluing the mind is also water from the spring of Zen teachings. In Zen, all tasks are equal, no matter how different they may be. These and other pearls of Zen wisdom have shaped this method, and are translated so that they can apply to the concrete realities of daily life, with all its responsibilities and challenges.

Contrary to what you may have subconsciously assumed, having picked up a book written by a Zen Buddhist, it's not necessary for you to actively meditate in order to use this method, although it will help you to better focus your attention and let go of things you no longer need. But the method itself will invite you to do this, too, and will also help you develop these qualities.

This doesn't mean I don't want to spark enthusiasm for meditation – on the contrary. Its focus, however, is different. With Zen, it's not so much about performing better as it is about becoming more transparent, less coloured by whatever it is you cling onto to provide yourself with an identity. It's a spiritual experience that doesn't want to be used deliberately because that would impose limitations. The spring needs to be able to flow. By using this method, though, you'll become familiar with the waters and flavour of Zen.

The fruits

Time Surfing gives you a permanent feeling of inner rest and mastery over your tasks. By following its simple instructions you know at any given moment where to direct your focus and also what you have to do in unforeseen circumstances.

Often, when you step out to take a breather, it will allow you to see the bigger picture and come up with good ideas about how to progress the task. Or it might be that the short time you've spent away from the project has shown you that switching to another task is the best route. Because you only do one thing at a time and you also know how to calm the worries in your head, you'll be able to execute all your tasks with a natural attention. You feel satisfied, not only when the job is finished, but especially when you're working on it.

Instead of being submerged by waves of small tasks and demands, you stand on top of the waves and feel yourself full of trust. In each moment, your intuition decides what should be done now, varying between important tasks and smaller tasks, between the creative ones and the "have-to-be dones".

Moreover, the intuition is taking care of your health and wellbeing. It will alternate your tasks in a good order and will also give you time for pleasant and comforting things to do.

PART I: TIME PRESSURE
WHY ARE WE STRESSED?

Faster and faster ...

When you watch a movie that was made 15 years ago, you realize how much our notion of time has changed. While it was common then for a camera to linger over a facial expression or focus on a curtain fluttering in the wind, nowadays it's all about fast-paced action that grabs hold from the start and doesn't let go until the credits roll. It's only when we see an old movie that we're suddenly aware of how we've gradually become used to the modern, faster pace of cinema – so much so that the older movies appear almost in slow motion.

Well, what is true for movies is just as true for our work and for how we spend much of our time. Here, as well, everything now moves at a much faster pace, but again we've gradually internalized this change and have come to see it as the norm.

It used to be that if you needed certain information, you had to put some effort into it, maybe spend an afternoon at the library. Nowadays, most information can be accessed with a few clicks of the mouse or taps on a smartphone. In fact, the situation has now reversed: instead of toiling away to try to find as much information as you can, there is now so much information available that you often have to decide what you don't need, because otherwise it becomes overwhelming. As a result, you choose selectively among instant online news sources, the daily paper and the more comprehensive weekly news magazines.

After a vacation, my father would always read his way through the newspapers that had piled up in our absence, much to the exasperation of my mother. "Do you really need to know all of that, Marcel?" she would ask. I don't

2

know whether it's the same for you, but fairly often I only look at the headlines on the front page, and then maybe at the comics or a favourite column in my daily newspaper.

In general, our communications are more fraught today than they used to be. We're expected to answer a WhatsApp message immediately, an email on the same day. These are the unwritten rules, and we feel more or less obliged to comply with them. Managing your email traffic without getting behind or letting your inbox clog up has become a true art form (see pages 133–8).

As well as the plethora of information it provides, the internet makes it possible for us to choose our own working hours. This brings with it the temptation to do some work in the evening as well – or even during vacations, as I do now during the fall school break in a cottage in Friesland, in the northern part of the Netherlands, surrounded by water and the children.

But, by allowing work to gradually infiltrate our time off, aren't we filling up our remaining chunks of free and available time in the same way city councils sacrifice the overgrown green play areas and undeveloped land to make way for useful buildings?

Is it even possible, we wonder, to operate from a place of calm? We're constantly juggling to keep all the balls in the air – if we slow down for even a moment, won't they all just fall to the ground?

In my practice, I regularly see people who struggle with this faster pace of life. Nurses, for example, worry that they have less and less time for each patient. What's more, they have to account for every second of it, logging every five minutes of activity into a computer program. The combination of these two things results in tension and feelings of inadequacy.

Entrepreneurs often tell me they post Tweets during their breaks and update their company Facebook page in the evening. They feel time pressure breathing down their neck constantly: if they don't keep moving, they'll be overtaken by someone else and fall behind.

Given all this evidence, it might seem obvious to view the acceleration of our workpace as the number one cause of stress. Indeed, I hear this a lot. Often people say to me: "You must have a lot of clients – who can keep up with this pace?"

But we humans are very adaptable animals. To keep up with the new pace we sacrifice part of our social life and instead communicate with our friends on Facebook or Twitter. We read fewer books. We watch less television. Hobbies? They're a thing of the past.

Not long ago, my family and I actually found ourselves putting together a jigsaw puzzle. Grandmother was visiting from Switzerland and had brought along a map of Amsterdam, which had been cut into 500 pieces and placed in an attractive tin. A friend joined us and we got started, first of all laying out the edge pieces, just like we used to do. Then we put together a few of the easier main streets and our own neighbourhood. "So relaxing!" we said. But that's as far as we got. A week later, I put the whole puzzle back in the tin. We don't have the time for that any more … It is not just the new, faster pace that makes us feel pressured for time, however. Even if the pace never got any faster, stress would still be lying in wait and we would still find it hard to operate from a place of calm.

For example, we are all guilty of putting off certain tasks, even though we know they're important. Most of us get irritated if someone interrupts us when we're concentrating, and we all get frustrated when we don't make any progress with our work because we're "having a bad day".

If we're not putting it off, we're busy just trying to "get it done" so that we can cross it off our list and move on to something else. Do we ever enjoy the work itself? Of course not. That liberating feeling that you experience when you finish something does not provide real satisfaction or, if it does, it's short-lived – before you know it, the next thing presents itself and then the whole cycle begins again.

We try to work more efficiently to save time, but the better we get at doing this, the more work we end up taking on.

We would like to have more control over our lives, to be able to carefully organize how we are going to get things done. Then we come up against the inevitable setbacks: an IT problem occurs; you have a sick child at home; there is ice on the roads; an emergency occurs. Or uninvited intruders invade, who grab our attention and turn our carefully laid plans upside down.

The tension these kinds of incidents produce is caused not by the faster pace, but primarily by the following two factors:

1. Wanting to manage our tasks with our heads (and thus be in control of when we have moments of calm).
2. Our inner rejection of things we see as unpleasant or as distractions (and, by extension, trying to keep out anything that might cause stress).

I'm a Zen monk, and as such I spend a lot of time intensively doing nothing. You'll often find me simply sitting on a cushion in a balanced posture, with my face to the wall. You might think that the recommendations of a Zen practitioner for finding a sense of calm would involve slowing down, meditating and returning to the way of life of an earlier time when everything was more peaceful, so let's have a closer look at these in turn.

Slowing down

Slowing down is indeed good advice, and can also be enjoyable. It can work particularly well with sensory activities, such as eating or taking a bath. But just try leisurely strolling around at work and you'll soon see that this is no easy task. Slowing down is only successful if it comes from within and is not imposed on you.

Meditation

Certain kinds of meditation and breathing exercises do result in fewer stress responses in the body. They can also be important tools for processing emotions, as we shall see later on. However, these exercises don't provide ways of preventing work-related stress.

Returning to an earlier time

The idea that things were less stressful in the past is a relative one. Many aspects of life in "the good old days" were far from peaceful. To be sure, my grandmother had time for the neighbours, wrote letters and regularly darned the holes in her family's socks. But she also had eight children, two of whom died, and a number of miscarriages. On Mondays, she washed the entire family's clothes by hand with the help of her eldest daughters. To keep the business going, her sons helped my grandfather make wooden shoes in his workshop. Life was hard, and it was often a matter of survival.

Just like Zen itself, the guidelines in this book are timeless. The starting point is not that we should aim to do *less*, but that whatever we do should arise from a place of calm.

Later on, we will see that a natural consequence of the method is that we filter out what really matters to us, allowing us to eliminate a number of tasks that are less important.

Before we begin to delve into the method of Time Surfing itself, let's first zoom out like Google Earth and get an overview of where "dealing with time" sits within the bigger picture of our lives.

As you're probably well aware, there are other reasons, unrelated to the number of tasks we have to do each day, that we feel stress and tension in our lives. It's helpful to know about and recognize them in order to be able to place Time Surfing within the proper context.

Stress from other domains: a four-storey house

Imagine a house with four levels: a basement, a ground floor, a first floor and a roof garden. When we are dealing with time, we are standing on the ground floor.

The ground floor

This is the floor where we live and where we carry out our daily activities – where we cook and eat, where we talk to our family and relax, where we work and play. And it's the subject of this book: how can you do all of these tasks with a sense of calm and satisfaction and not feel pressured, hurried and tense? Our day-to-day wellbeing, therefore, is determined largely on the ground floor.

The basement

Below the ground floor is the basement, which is where our emotions live, and it is the foundation beneath the house. You can think of your emotions as your body's ancient but extremely useful communication system. Together, it's as if emotions form an ocean that's always flowing underneath our skin, using waves to communicate all kinds of signals to us. These can be emotionally positive, such as love for our children or happiness when we are surrounded by friends, or they can be negative – warning us of imminent danger or helping us to deal with loss. Emotions guide us to come to terms with our current situation, good or bad – that is, if we give the emotion the chance to do this and don't reject it.

When we try to use our thoughts to neutralize an emotional reaction such as fear ("Come on, there's no need to be afraid of the exam, you can do it ... "), we suppress the emotion and cause the system to short-circuit, as it were. What we should actually do is allow ourselves to really *feel* the emotion rather than resist it. Then the fear/grief/sadness/frustration will disappear on its own. This often doesn't happen, however, either because we'd rather avoid really engaging with negative emotions or we simply don't know how to.

The theme of emotions will occasionally surface in the method that follows, when they might be the cause of what I refer to as "gnawing rats". These are the things in your life that you put off and which then start to "gnaw" at you. For example, when you avoid having a conversation with someone because you're intimidated by their authority or are afraid of a negative reaction, this "gnawing rat" is caused by an emotion: fear.

The things we worry about in the back of our minds (whether the children are safe, if you're going to be able to make it financially, if you're suffering from a serious disease ...), referred to as "background programs" in this book, are emotional in nature.

The first floor

The floor directly above the ground floor is the domain of the self-image.

Our self-image is the relationship we have with ourselves. If this relationship is healthy, it means we have a natural self-confidence and are generally glad to be alive. We have a resilient spirit and find our place in the world with ease. We also know how to be gentle with ourselves when it comes to our shortcomings and the mistakes we make.

For the most part, our self-image is formed in our youth, and is so powerful that it is passed on to our adult self virtually intact. If we were often criticized as a child, or were pressured to conform to our parents' expectations while perhaps being compared to a sibling whom they saw as a higher achiever, we will have developed negative thoughts about ourselves as a result. As adults, we still think we're not very good, or at least not compared to others. We can also become obsessed with trying to get from others the recognition we're unable to give to ourselves.

Our self-image can affect how we deal with time, the theme of this book. It leans down over the balcony and gives orders to the ground floor: "Can't you go a little faster?" "Are you really doing your best?" "Are you getting the recognition you deserve?"

The roof garden

The top floor – the roof garden – is out in the open. This is where we make our wishes known to the rest of the world and where we set boundaries with others. It's where we communicate and share things.

We're clearly visible to other people on the roof garden, and it's good if this doesn't bother us and we even make sure that others can see us. If we do this, people will take us into consideration and not create problems for us unintentionally.

If we don't, we'll get the impression that others are just walking all over us and that we're constantly having to adapt ourselves to our partner, our neighbours and our co-workers. This irritation can then ultimately lead to an outburst, which might be out of all proportion. There's an art to broaching a sensitive issue, and this involves a number of distinct qualities that you can learn and practise. An important aspect of this is that you know how to deal with the fact that you feel hurt by the other

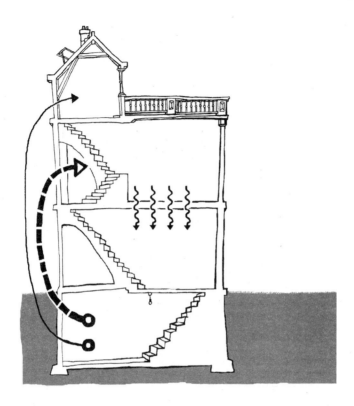

person. You have to come to terms with it, which was the theme of the basement of the house. In this way, all four floors are interconnected.

The walls of the house: The tension in your body

As well as the four themes mentioned above, there is one more aspect to be aware of that is just as important. In terms of the house metaphor, it's not a floor, but rather the material the house is made from.

These are the physical reactions to stress that your body uses if it needs to put on the brakes. Usually, you only think about taking steps to deal with stress when it starts to affect you physically. Stress can cause a variety of complaints. Some claim that the majority of diseases and health conditions can be put down to stress.

In the absence of stress, our body has a robust immune system that functions well and protects us against health problems. Animals that can roam around freely – such as cats that spend a lot of time outdoors – are seldom sick. When you learn to relax and breathe properly, or if you practise some form of meditation, this strengthens your immune system.

Often we are unaware that we hold tension in certain parts of our bodies. Most of us tense our shoulders or hold our stomach in. We also allow ourselves to remain on high alert, as a precaution or out of habit. Our alarm system is always switched part-way on. The consequences of this near-constant tension only become apparent years later. It is possible, though, to change your habits by reminding your body to be aware of what it's doing.

For now, however, let's return to the ground floor ...

MY OWN EXPERIENCES

Lists

The Time Surfing method came to me, one instruction after the other, during an experiment I conducted on myself at a time when I was more stressed than I cared to be. It was the spring of 2005. I was at that time working as an actor and a director, and was involved in a succession of projects that at times would overlap (something that is not uncommon in this line of work). At one point, for example, I found myself directing a circus in Switzerland and performing in a show for young audiences that was touring the Netherlands. At the same time, I was also responsible for the European Zen Center in Amsterdam, not to mention the father of a family with small children. Our youngest had what she called "nightfears" during this time, and would often come and snuggle up next to my wife and I in bed. The morning alarm seemed to go off terribly early in those days.

With so much on my plate, I was terrified I was going to forget some vital job I had to do or accidentally miss a deadline. So that this wouldn't happen, I had come up with an ingenious system of lists. There were three categories: work, Zen and home. Each category was divided into sections. I could print the lists straight from the computer, complete with the appropriate headings. There were extra spaces for new items. In this way I could always see what I'd already done and checked off the list. But, more than anything, I could also see what I had yet to do – and this made me nervous, because there was always a lot left on the list. It was like playing a game of Tetris. I'd be relieved when I saw a couple of the bottom rows disappear, but then these would be replaced by new blocks from above, which fell even faster. It was endless.

Some of the stress inside my head came from always being able to see how much I still had to do. Some of it was there because I unconsciously wished that this runaway train would stop so I could just be done. And, of course, also because it really was a lot.

I was a Zen monk. Where was my sense of calm, my tranquillity, I wondered? I was tense, tired and worried. It was during this period that an idea gradually started to take shape. I decided to take up the challenge. I gathered up all of my lists and saw once again how wonderfully detailed and perfect they were. And then I tore them up and threw them away.

Observing

This marked the start of my research into the causes of stress. Deciding to throw away the lists seemed ridiculous and rash. But the idea behind it was sound: by doing so, I was removing a major source of stress. Taking this rigorous intuitive step forced me to go back to square one and figure out where I'd lost my sense of calm and how I could get it back – for good. It wasn't so much a matter of being able to find a sense of calm now and then – I realized that this had to be the starting point. *Everything I did* had to come from a place of calm and balance.

Zen meditation served me well during this experiment. Among other things, Zen trains you to observe. You sit quietly and, whether it's hot or cold, pleasant or painful, silent or noisy, you don't move. During meditation, you observe the slightest changes, not just those around you but also those inside of you, both in your body and in your mind. And because you don't do anything with them, because you don't act on them and don't have anywhere to go, you remain largely objective as an observer. You're not looking for anything. Your observations aren't coloured by what you would like to see. I realized that Zen had provided me with a precision instrument, a sensitive and exceptionally useful barometer.

Observing tension

For instance, during meditation, I would sometimes feel tightness in my belly. My breathing would become less regular. I wouldn't be able to let go of this right away. Sometimes it would disappear at the end of the meditation, but then the next time it might return.

So I asked myself, where did this tightness come from? I expanded my observations to include daily life. I was often amazed to find that, without my being aware of it, I had tightened my stomach muscles. This tightness would arise and then subside again – for example, during and after a telephone call. Sometimes it would get stuck. Then, on other occasions, it would seem as if there were opposing forces at work, some kind of internal resistance that would form a barrier and keep the tightness from dissipating. This would happen if something was bothering me but I wasn't able to talk about it. Or if I was apprehensive about something.

This was interesting. By paying attention to how my stomach muscles responded, I could observe my unconscious reactions. They revealed what my mind was doing.

No lists

Because I was no longer making lists, I operated entirely according to what I could remember – only the appointments I made went on the calendar. I would remember the really important things, I thought naïvely.

Because of the unusual situation I had deliberately placed myself in, I started to make some discoveries. So as not to forget anything, I paid special attention to the reminders my mind was sending me. I became aware when something from within was asking for my attention. And that could come at inconvenient moments. I was just starting to focus on learning my lines for a play, for example, when a voice inside me said: "Don't forget to make an appointment with the dental hygienist ... "

Why had that voice come barging in now, right at the moment my mind was focusing on something else? It bothered me. And so I said to the thought: "Go away. Bring me your message at a better time."

Meanwhile, my barometer started to sound the alarm: it had detected tension, physical tension. Because I felt harassed, I had also rejected the reminder with my muscles. Rejection causes tension, I concluded.

I also noticed other things, which I was only able to do because I'd done away with my lists. I relied more and more on my gut feelings. With increasing frequency, I was doing things when I was in the mood to do them. In other words, when I allowed myself to follow my gut I was much more likely to do things at the right moment, and then enjoy all of the advantages this brought with it.

The instructions for installing a new wireless modem, I found, are much easier to understand if you read them at the right moment, when you're feeling rested. Making a difficult phone call at the right moment can mean you're able to steer things in the right direction or find a solution to a problem you'd been grappling with.

Or, conversely, if I felt inspired, I could now act on this immediately, even if it came at an odd moment. For example, one evening, after a long drive, I wrote out the first draft of a talk, simply because it felt like a good time to do it.

"The right moment" became a new concept for me, and other new concepts would follow.

Intuition

What I was really doing when I listened to my gut was making choices intuitively.

Up until then, for me, like for so many others, the concept of intuition had been a vague one, something that existed but which was unreliable. Intuition was used mainly by women, I thought, while men were better at reading maps. Women were about feelings. Men, the big picture. Intuition was about sensing what was yet to come, and being able to see beyond what was visible on the surface. By calling it intuition, all sorts of otherwise unverifiable claims could be made.

Now that I was using my gut feelings to navigate time, I had to admit that in fact I was using my intuition. There was no map available for what I was doing. And it went even further. I also inadvertently investigated exactly how intuition works and what conditions need to be in place to allow yourself to really trust it. (For the record, I observed that this worked just as well in men as in women!)

But, as my students often ask: "When you choose what you're going to do intuitively, don't you then mainly do the things you like to do and ignore the ones you don't?"

The question seems justified, and stems from our own experience: we don't feel like doing chores that are boring (paperwork) or unpleasant (cleaning the cat's litter tray). We do them because we have to. However, intuition is also good at dealing with things we have to do!

In fact, there's a more subtle reason your intuition doesn't choose to do something. As I've said, I chose tasks using my intuition, and I found that the things that did not present themselves to me – the things I therefore forgot – turned out to be precisely those things I had rejected inwardly earlier on. My intuition did not invite me to actually make the appointment with the dental hygienist because I had turned away from it.

I concluded that the intuition notices only the things you have a positive relationship with – anything else will fly under the radar. That sounds both simple and logical, doesn't it? The criterion for remembering to do something intuitively is not whether something is difficult or unpleasant, therefore – it's whether it's *real* for you, whether you've created an honest relationship with it.

During those first few weeks, there were a lot of things that I had managed to forget – some minor, some considerably more serious ... After some consideration, I reluctantly returned to using a list, something I had developed such an aversion to. However, there was one important change: I no longer used lists to determine what I had to do, but instead it acted as a checklist for me to see if I'd forgotten anything. And I also used it to check whether the system was functioning properly.

What I now know is that, over time, the more the new system is integrated into the old (read: the more you dare to trust it), the less you need the list. Once you're accustomed to using the method, you hardly forget a thing.

Right now, I only use a list if I'm extremely busy. And even then, as I say, I only use it as a check, because it's especially during these very busy times that the method proves itself to be so effective. Under the sound guidance of your intuition, you're able to complete one task after the other, and, even better, the precision with which your intuition governs your actions gets you to do the right thing at the right time.

The longer I used the new method, the more I began to realize that the benefits it offered went further than just the sense of calm I was seeking. This method was good not only for my inner wellbeing, but also for managing my schedule and improving the quality of my work.

My intuition was a better manager than my mind. More sensitive, more flexible – and deeper. But I did have to provide it with the right information. In that respect, it was just as demanding as my mind. It wanted to know everything about everything that had to be done. And I had to make sure I didn't withhold any information, or present it in a negative way.

My experiment led to a change greater than the one I'd anticipated. I'd switched drivers! The old one was called control and overview. The new one was called intuition, and the fuel it required was trust.

The blueprint

After about a month, a kind of blueprint developed inside my head, one which was in place before I was actually able to confirm everything in practice. I sometimes had doubts about my own discoveries. For example, when my head was too full. Then I would get a piece of paper, write everything down and work my way through a list.

All done.

But the next day I would start using the new method again. I figured out that the only reason there were so many things in my head was because I didn't really dare to trust the method. A sense of calm arises when you hand over the controls completely to your intuition and trust it won't forget anything. What I was doing was peeking out from behind the door with my mind so that I could stay in control to some extent. And my head got tired.

The idea of "the breather" – a kind of regular mini-break – came up before I realized how valuable it really was and started using it consistently. Now these breathers feel natural, and my body asks for them, as it were. In the beginning, I allowed myself to be trapped by the computer, and sat glued to my chair doing one thing after another. But I started to understand ever more deeply that the entire method hinges on the breather. By putting it into practice, I discovered the many benefits it had to offer, which were more than I ever suspected at the start. The further I got, the longer I used the method, the more the blueprint revealed itself to me. It consisted of a number of principles that, just like the organs of our bodies, formed a single whole. I started to count these principles. There could have been six of them, or eight. But I was pleasantly surprised to find there were seven.

It is not a list of hints that can be added to endlessly.

These seven elements go together, and you could say that one leads to the other. They belong together. They're blood relatives. And when they're all working as one, the family is complete.

The name

I still needed a name. Over and over, the blueprint proved to be accurate. It was a natural system. It needed a name that clearly expressed what it was all about. I thought about that other widely known way of dealing with the things you need to do: time management. With time management, you try to use time to your advantage by thinking things through, thereby allowing your mind to decide whether something is important or not.

What we're talking about here is trust, not control. Managing time isn't left to the mind, but to the intuition. Being attuned to time, allowing it to ripen, trusting your intuition, using what emerges.

It's like surfing. Surfing with sensitivity and finesse over the ever-changing waves of time. Time Surfing.

PART II: THE METHOD
THE SEVEN INSTRUCTIONS IN BRIEF

Instruction 1

do one thing at a time and finish what you're doing

Rather than multitasking, always complete a job before going on to the next.

Instruction 2

Be aware of what you're doing and accept it

By marking the start of an activity, you can then embrace what you're doing.

Instruction 3

Create breathers between activities

Alternate times of focused attention with moments when you release the focus.

Instruction 4
Give your full attention to drop-ins, creating a relationship with everything you want to do
When something unexpected happens, take it seriously rather than rejecting it.

Instruction 5
Become aware of "gnawing rats" and transform them into "white sheep"
"Gnawing rats" are things you put off. Befriend them, and they will then turn into "white sheep". Sheep follow quietly behind the shepherd and don't keep him awake at night.

Instruction 6
Observe background programs
These are thoughts that keep going through your head because you're worried or feel hurt. They can suck up a lot of energy. Calm them down.

Instruction 7
Use your intuition when choosing what to do
Your intuition is your best planner. If you trust it, it will provide you with a solid foundation of calm.

IN THE BEGINNING

The previous pages set out the seven instructions in brief. Now we will explore each of them in greater detail. To thoroughly familiarize yourself with the method and put it into practice, I recommend using the same sequence. Try first to get an overview by taking in the short descriptions, and then focus on each aspect individually.

As with anything new, it's a good idea to be patient with yourself when you're starting out. If you want to learn how to play chess, you first need to learn how the different pieces move. Some of these moves – such as the knight's ability to jump – might seem strange at first, and only start to feel familiar with practice. Others, like the way the rook moves over the horizontal and vertical rows, are simple and seem obvious even at the very start. Getting the pieces to work together optimally results in a good game. And this method is no different. Some of the instructions speak for themselves and you can integrate them immediately.

Others will take more time to master, so you'll need to be patient.

The instruction that deals with what I refer to as "gnawing rats" – the things you put off – might result in even more agitation to start with. Don't be alarmed. It's only when you focus on them that you notice just how many gnawing rats you're feeding. It's not possible to befriend all of the rats at once, and you'll meet them one by one. Over time, things will settle down here as well. Because you're taking a different approach to your tasks, this at least means no new gnawing rats will be showing up to join the line. You befriend them as soon as they come in the door, so to speak.

As I have already mentioned, trusting the method is an important precondition. This means you no longer need to constantly see everything there right in front of you.

For example, when you've made sure your intuition knows you want to make an appointment with the dental hygienist, you can then let it go – in other words, forget about it! In fact, you have to let it go, because this is precisely what provides you with a sense of calm. Your intuition will take care of things from here on out, and it will choose the right moment to make that phone call.

The longer you use the method, the easier it gets. That's true for many things, but it's especially true for Time Surfing. You're not learning something that's difficult and new – you're returning to what comes naturally. This is why, over time, the instructions will no longer be necessary: you'll be doing it already, on your own.

INSTRUCTION 1:

DO ONE THING AT A TIME, AND FINISH WHAT YOU'RE DOING

Explanation

Choose one thing as your main task right now. Don't have all kinds of different files open simultaneously as you work on them a little at a time.

And don't try to multitask. If you run a bicycle repair store, either serve a client or put a new chain on a bicycle, but don't do both things at once. If you're making a meal in the evening, either stir whatever you're cooking or talk with a friend on the phone – don't start doing one until you've finished the other.

Do one thing at a time. You can forget about all the rest. They'll get their turn later on.

Example

Our days are made up of separate activities that, in turn, each become the main activity of the present moment: you travel to work, you talk with a co-worker, you answer your email, you're in a meeting, you design something, you go out for a walk, you write an article.

A day at home might look like this: you straighten up the living room, you load the washing machine, you play with the dog, you read a chapter of your book, you go grocery shopping. You do one thing after the other, always doing one thing at a time.

Commentary

Ask yourself which things you already do from a place of calm and with pleasure. Have a look at the various parts of your life – work, home life and free time – and answer this question before reading on.

There's a good chance you came up with things like cooking, playing sports, gardening or being on your own at work when no one can interrupt you.

If you look for the common denominator, you'll notice that whatever it is, you're doing just that one thing with no interruptions. It doesn't have to be done in a hurry, there are no other urgent matters waiting for you, and you're not constantly being distracted by people who want something from you. What's more, you've chosen this task or activity of your own free will. The simple act of doing just one thing means that it is calming and enjoyable. How wonderful it would be if we could experience this with everything we did!

So let's take this as both our starting point and our first instruction. Then we'll investigate what conditions would need to occur for us to be able to experience this feeling of calm with everything we do.

Don't multitask

The first instruction can best be explained by telling you what not to do – namely, multitasking. Today, scientists define multitasking not, as the name might suggest, as doing multiple tasks at once, but the act of rapidly switching back and forth between tasks. So, theoretically, it's not even possible to do two things at once – so how is it that we seem to do it all the time?

We listen to a radio programme while we're driving the car, or talk on the phone *Do things* while we're straightening up the *one after the* living room, or chat to our spouse *other instead* while we chop vegetables. You *of all at once* might have had the experience of biking or driving home when you suddenly realize that, although you've been lost in thought for a large part of the journey, you still managed to make the right turns, stop at the red lights and didn't get into (or cause) any accidents. You were doing two things – driving and thinking about what to buy your brother for his birthday next week – at the same time. Right? Look closely, however, and you'll see all of these examples have one thing in common: one of the two activities was being carried out on autopilot, almost unconsciously.

When an activity has become second nature to us and we no longer have to think about what we're doing, we can easily do something else at the same time. Until … we suddenly have to brake for the car in front of us and quickly try to gain an overview of the new situation that's arisen – and then, when things have settled down again, we notice we've missed part of that interesting radio programme.

When we need to focus our attention on something, we do just that one thing. If we need to give our attention to both things, it means we're sacrificing something in the process.

Eating

Eating alone feels like a solitary affair. But things change when you go through the pile of newspapers and pull out a magazine. You push your plate to one side, put the magazine on the other. Let the fun begin. As you read, you keep missing the shrimp with your fork, and occasionally even miss your mouth. You're amazed at how quickly you've emptied your plate. You haven't even really tasted your food. If you were to read through a list of ingredients you'd just consumed, you'd notice that most of them had passed you by. You have a rough idea of the general flavour of the dish, but haven't really tasted anything specific. When you focus on reading, you cannot simultaneously focus on taste. You can only focus on one thing at a time.

The same thing also happens when you have a meal with others. At the high point of the conversation, when people are joking around or sharing stories from the past, you're also doing only one thing at a time. You're paying attention to the stories, and so you can't also focus your attention on the taste of the fish or wine. To do this, you'll need to pause for a moment and take the time to notice what the food in front of you smells like, to hold the sip of wine in your mouth and focus entirely on the sense perceptions of your nose and tongue.

Talking on the phone

Talking on the telephone seems like something that uses only half of your abilities. One hand is busy, and the other hand is not. Moreover, the other person can't see what you're doing, and so it's not just possible to do something else with the other hand, it won't cause any offence if you do. At home, it happens almost automatically: you answer the phone and then tidy up the living room or load the washing machine as you talk.

In such cases, it doesn't affect the intensity of the conversation that much. You can straighten up the living room or load the washing machine without having to think about it. It's different for things that do require your attention, however.

If you're on the phone and you have your email program opened in front of you on your laptop, the temptation to start scrolling through your emails during the call is huge. If the person on the other end is doing so, you can tell very quickly that you're not getting their full attention. It will even cause some irritation because it feels as if you're not worth their time. During a phone call it's better, therefore, to close your laptop or stand up in order to avoid this temptation, allowing you to stay focused on the conversation. It will probably go a lot faster and be much more effective as a result.

You naturally pay attention when you do one thing at a time. You taste your food, you're aware of the other person, you know what you're doing. It's one of the important keys to a sense of calm. Your mind settles down because you know which task you're doing, and realize that the others will get their turn later on. Your work itself also becomes calm because you are focusing on only one thing. Rather than saving time, doing several things at once in fact takes longer because of the agitation and loss of attention it brings with it.

Finish what you're doing

"Finish what you're doing" is the last part of an activity. Children find this hard. It's no longer constructive, creative and fun. It involves putting things away. And that's boring! Much unnecessary stress results from neglecting this final aspect of an activity. In the form of Zen that I practise, it's an essential part of the training and is practised during *samu*, working selflessly for the group.

During one of the first Zen summer camps I took part in, I was approached by Isabelle, a wiry and exceptionally lively Frenchwoman, who asked if I might like to help out at the bar. I said yes. It sounded like fun, and I could also get to know people in the process. Things got under way after the evening meditation session in a see-through tunnel-like tent, out in nature, near a lake in the woods. We worked non-stop. After *zazen*,* 150 people all arrived for refreshments at the same time, and those of us who were serving them could barely manage to keep up. The next day, after morning meditation, I enjoyed some well-earned rest by going for a walk in the woods.

---

* Seated meditation on a cushion in a straight and concentrated posture with the legs crossed. A session usually consists of two 35-minute sessions, with a slow, five-minute walk called *kinhin* in between.

A little later I saw Isabelle again and she asked where I'd been. It turned out that the bar was cleaned in the morning by the same crew who'd served the night before. I was embarrassed by my extravagant mistake. In Zen, completing a task is even more important than sharing the work equally.

When something is finished, it settles down. And so do we. So finish things. During a work-related conversation or meeting, matters are often discussed that you want to remember later on. The best time to make notes on this is right after the talk. It's a way for you to round things off. If you've repaired something in the house, the final step is to put away the tools and clean up the mess. Don't immediately move on to the next thing, but first take a "breather", a short break of a few minutes (Instruction 3).

Of course, you don't have to finish larger tasks or jobs in one go – these can be divided up into sections in a way that feels natural. For all of these sections you use the instruction "finish what you're doing". This is how a painting, a project or the interior of a house comes into being: one layer at a time.

BE AWARE OF WHAT YOU'RE DOING AND ACCEPT IT

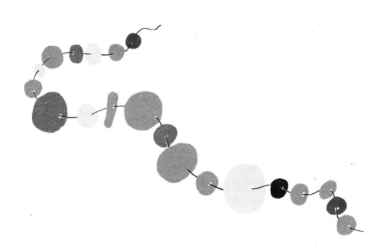

Explanation

The second instruction involves taking a moment to realize that the task or activity you've chosen is your only task at this very moment.

You do this by becoming consciously aware of this fact, preferably at the start of the activity. For the first few weeks, it is useful to internally "name" the activity – "I am making breakfast for my children" – until the awareness comes naturally. By using this instruction, every action, large or small, will be permeated with natural attention.

Fully accept every activity as your task for this moment. Embrace it, no matter what it is. All the while, remember to remain natural and flexible. It shouldn't require any strength to focus your attention on the activity.

Example

As you're starting a task, consciously choose this to be your main activity at this moment.

You arrive at work, and at the beginning of the morning you're going to meet with a co-worker. You bring a moment of awareness to the task: "I'm starting my meeting with Suzanne."

When the meeting is over and you're about to write up your notes, you bring awareness to the moment: "I'm going to write up the report." You then take a short break and say to yourself: "I'm taking a breather."

Your next activity might be drawing up a quote. You confirm your choice: "I'm going to prepare a quote."

You do the same thing at home, taking a moment to become aware of every new activity: "I'm taking a shower," "I'm making a meal," "I'm cleaning."

You do this not only with the more substantial activities, but also with the smaller ones: "I'm emptying the dishwasher," "I'm making the bed," "I'm cleaning the cat's litter tray." In this way, you ensure that they are elevated to the main task of the moment.

Commentary

"Be aware of what you're doing" is an instruction in which you can feel the presence of Zen. By choosing just one thing and forgetting about the rest, a natural attention for what you're doing arises of its own accord. Moreover, it means that you're consciously choosing what you're going to do and aren't just putting out fires and being a slave to your work.

If you look at the day's activities as a string of beads, you will see it's made up of all different kinds: large, weighty beads and small, carefully painted ones; eye-catching multicoloured beads and unassuming, softly coloured ones. Which kind of bead is most important to you? Your morning shower? Or the meeting with a client? The moment of relaxing during which you have a bright idea? Or the time you spend playing with your children?

When viewed from the broad perspective of time, all beads are equally important. They're all pieces of our lives.

"I sometimes feel as if everything that truly matters can be contained in a single moment that captures the essence of life, and we've still got all the time in the world for that."

Pauline, my first wife, wrote this in a letter to her friend Joost. They both had cancer. Joost was struggling terribly, and Pauline wanted to encourage him. This sentence made such an impression on me when I read it and it's stayed with me ever since. She was probably able to understand and realize this truth because she was directly facing her own mortality.

A day is made up of beads of time that we string together, and we can bring them to life to a greater or lesser degree.

We have three cats in our family. Because we don't want to have a cat flap, I am often opening the kitchen door to let them out. This allows me to observe how a cat marks the transition between inside and outside. Paris, the naughtiest of the trio, leisurely stretches back first one leg and then the other. Then he goes and stands right in the middle of the doorway, so you can't close the door. He looks around a bit, and just when you start to think:

"Are you going out or aren't you?" he strides majestically into the back garden. With this, he demonstrates precisely what is meant by the second instruction.

It is by marking the transition before each new activity that you *Mark the* will start to see that your string *transition* is made up of individual beads. This in turn makes it easier to devote yourself entirely to whatever you're doing at the present moment.

As mentioned earlier, consciously naming the activity you intend to carry out can help you create this awareness, but this will become unnecessary over time. As you become accustomed to Time Surfing, you'll notice that you welcome every new task or activity as a matter of course, and naming will become redundant. Doing one thing at a time is part of our natural default mode as human beings, and if you even point yourself in this direction, it's as if your body recognizes this behaviour and embraces it with open arms.

Rushing

Rushing is an example of the opposite: unnatural behaviour. And, no matter how unhealthy and unpleasant it may be, there's a good chance we start our day by rushing around. It's as if we try to compress the number of things we have to do at that moment into a time frame that's too limited. Within a short period of time we get dressed, brush our teeth, shower, have breakfast, gather our things together and, if we can't find something, curse inwardly with one eye on the clock. When there are children in the mix – who might be determined to wear the wrong clothes for the time of year or who accidentally knock over a cup of tea, and for whom hurrying is no fun at all – the conditions are ripe for a morning storm.

In general, we tend to hurry when doing things that can be seen as preparation for what comes next. These are activities like travelling to work, preparing the room before a meeting or doing the grocery shopping for the weekend. What comes next is more important. In our eyes, that's what matters.

Rushing is like gulping down time. You're not living for now but for later. When we rush, we might sacrifice whole clusters of little beads for another, shinier or heavier bead.

Accept yourself at the start of the day

It's much more pleasant for both you and the day you're beginning to do the opposite – namely, to take your time in the morning. In many spiritual traditions, this is seen as an ideal time for meditation or looking inward. Such a moment of calm and stillness affects the rest of the day.

You can do this very simply while having a cup of tea or coffee. Choose a pleasant spot in your home, and don't do anything but feel the warmth of the cup and drink the tea. Don't turn on the radio or read. You will then be able to feel your body as it is right now, on this morning. It might feel energetic and eager to get started, or it might still feel tired and heavy after a bad night's sleep. In the latter case: don't fight it, and don't reject either tiredness or pain. Accept your body exactly as it is at that moment. During those few minutes with your cup of tea, put on your body like you would put on a glove. If you make a habit of this, you'll start to look forward to this moment of being with yourself, and you'll be able to find time for it at other points during the day as well. What's more, this will get you off to a good start, and set the tone for accepting whatever it is you're doing as the main activity of the moment.

Travel time

Travelling is another activity that's easy to see as secondary, a lead-up to the "main event" that lies at the destination. Some people always wait until the last minute to leave, which means they're always travelling in a rush.

But travelling can be far more than purely functional. Take advantage of the fact that you're out and about for a while. You're in the fresh air and can feel the sun, rain or wind on your skin. You meet people, you see the cherry blossoms, you hear a blackbird singing – the world is full of delights to draw your attention. And best of all … you're with yourself!

At the same time, travelling is also a natural way of taking a break – it functions as a breather, as we will see in the next instruction. So, take *Turn an interlude into the main event* your time while you travel, and rather than seeing it as something that merely gets you to the next activity, turn this interlude into the main event of the moment.

Attention

What is natural attention? Can you still think about other things at the same time? The word "natural" implies that

41

you don't have to force yourself to stay focused on the matter at hand. Time Surfing allows your attention to focus naturally on what you're doing, and it's not disruptive if you let your thoughts wander along the way.

Once, a participant in my course came up to me after we'd covered this instruction the previous week. She told me she found it very tiring to think of nothing else while biking. I had to laugh, but was also grateful for her remark, because it showed how this instruction can be misinterpreted. She pointed out what happens when you try to force yourself to pay attention: you get tired. It's also unnecessary. When you do one thing at a time and consciously choose to do this, the activity becomes meaningful for you. Attention arises naturally. So it's fine if your thoughts wander while you're biking or walking to work.

Thoughts cannot be controlled, not even during meditation. It's actually good if you're relaxed and natural. When a situation calls for it – for example, when you're crossing a road – you'll focus your attention specifically on this.

This will also happen when you experience something wonderful, such as when you taste your grandmother's cherry jam or when a child runs up and throws their arms around you. You'll then experience these moments with heightened attention. Such things are pleasurable and are the spice of life. We'll speak more about this, what I term the "icing on the cake", later on.

We'll also see that, when it comes to feelings, it can be helpful to sharpen your focus and to pay attention to your body. When you experience an emotion, it's as if the body is sending out a message to you and wants to be heard. At such times, just thinking about the emotion is not enough. It is one of the things "mindfulness training" focuses on: feeling with awareness. This theme will be covered in Instruction 6, "Observe background programs".

Accept what you're doing

What we're talking about here is accepting not only that you're starting something new, but also fully accepting what the task at hand involves. Accepting this is a small step, but one that makes all the difference. Instead of being mainly preoccupied with the future, you consciously turn your attention toward the present moment, and no matter what the activity may be, you place it centre stage in the scene that you're in. Then you do this one thing and forget about all the rest. In this regard, it doesn't matter if what you're doing is important and potentially has a lot riding on it, or whether it's something small that no one can see or particularly values. It's relatively easy to give interesting or creative activities a leading role. But we might find it difficult to accept and become absorbed in a number of other tasks, such as those that are monotonous or dirty.

Elevate monotonous tasks to an art form

Monotonous tasks

In the courses I give, participants often mention ironing as a job they dislike. You can classify it under recurring household chores such as vacuuming, loading the dishwasher, folding the laundry, and so on. Rather than being necessarily boring, however, often we develop an aversion to them precisely because we think we have more important things to do. But if we accept them as the only activity of this very moment, they suddenly gain an entirely new meaning.

I can still see my grandmother sitting at the kitchen table peeling potatoes with a small paring knife. No one could match her speed and skill. With her large family, countless kilos of potatoes had flown through her fingers. As a child, I noticed that when my grandmother peeled potatoes, it became something beautiful. I would watch, spellbound, as the potatoes danced in her hands.

When we become one with our movements, they take on elegance. You can also see this when you watch a craftsperson at work. Their expertise transforms their work into artistry and them into an artist.

I once saw a documentary about a professional ironer. As I watched him work, I got the same feeling I used to get when I watched my grandmother peeling those potatoes. The way his hands guided the iron, pressing the shirts with swift, smooth strokes, was beautiful to behold.

If you embrace these kinds of tasks, they become pleasant. And, what's more, they become relaxing.

Dirty jobs

As well as the monotonous, there is yet another category of tasks we might find unpleasant. These are the dirty and the hard jobs, like cleaning the toilet or emptying the cat's litter tray, unclogging a blocked drain or taking out the garbage. Does this mean that some of the beads on our string are dirty, too?

Doing something fully brings fulfilment

"You have to define the moment you'll do it," said one participant. That's one option. However, I would suggest something else: you have to accept it. Before you start, you can say to yourself: "I accept this activity." Then you get out the cleaning products and perform the task with patience and care.

Fulfilment

Etymologically speaking, the word fulfilment contains the words "full" and "fill". Making full – doing fully. Our ancestors equated becoming completely absorbed in something with fulfilment or a sense of satisfaction. This is the precious gift that falls into our lap when we put the first two instructions into practice. You feel satisfied, not only when the job is finished, but especially when you're doing the work. You experience this time and again, one bead after the other, whether it happens to be a large, weighty bead or a small, unassuming one.

INSTRUCTION 3:
CREATE BREATHERS BETWEEN ACTIVITIES

Explanation

Take a short break, or "breather", after about 40 minutes, or when your attention wanes. Take one when you finish a task as well.

During a breather, you let your mind roam free. This doesn't necessarily mean you take a rest or do nothing, unless your job involves physical labour. A good definition of a breather is doing something that requires no mental effort. For example, washing out a few cups. By doing so, you distract your mind, and it's free to spin around and make associations. By allowing your mind to unwind in this way, you actually create room for brain waves and flashes of inspiration. In Instruction 7 you'll make use of these.

Example

You've taken a series of photographs and want to make a selection for an album or presentation. You look through the photos and indicate the ones you want to use and the ones you want to delete. This job takes half an hour.

You get up and take a breather: you make yourself a cup of tea. While doing this, you remember that you still want to return your friend Hannah's call. It also occurs to you that a particular photo could be wonderful if you cropped it. You call Hannah. Then you go back to what you were doing, look through all of the photos again, and arrange the best ones in a separate folder. You crop the photo and then edit a few others.

After a while, things aren't going quite as smoothly. You get up and unload the dishwasher. Then you make a sandwich. You decide what you'd like to make for dinner tonight. Then you realize that a photo you'd decided not to use was special and worth including after all. When you pick up where you left off, you add this one to the photos you selected.

Commentary

Emptiness provides contrast to form. In the same way, the time we spend not working is vital to the time we spend being productive. Vacations, weekends, our free evenings: they provide us with the resilience and energy we need to be able to work well.

This principle is just as important on weekdays. Not only in the form of a lunch break, but breaks throughout the day. I call these brief pauses between activities "breathers". We will see that the function of a breather goes beyond simply providing a moment of calm. While most of our time is filled in, during a breather it's just the opposite. For a short period of time, you allow yourself to clean the slate. Everything has a beginning and an end, and we have a reason for doing everything. A breather leaves this all behind for a moment, and by doing so makes way for a wondrous but logical phenomenon.

When you're on a train and looking out at the passing landscape, it doesn't take long before you're musing about all sorts of things. Your thoughts have free rein. You're neither in A, where you've come from, nor in B, where you're heading. And this gives your mind the chance to gain an overview. You're speeding not only over the rails, but also over your life as it is right now. From this vantage point, your mind starts to make connections. It notices how you've changed – perhaps you'll realize you're more determined in your approach than before. Or you think about work, and see the effect a conversation with a co-worker had on the quality of the report you recently completed. When you're in one place, whether it's A or B, it's not as easy to notice changes. Distance provides perspective.

You can also see this when it comes to noticing children's growth and development. Uncles and aunts immediately exclaim how much the children have grown lately, while as a parent you don't notice it so much. You're too close. You need distance to fully appreciate the changes. And that's exactly what a breather provides.

Taking a breather actually saves time

Here is a short summary of the instructions we've covered up until now, using the imagery of the string of beads:

1. Choose consciously one bead at a time.
2. Perceive and experience this string of time, bead after bead. And now:
3. Create space between the beads.

A breather is defined not only as taking a short break (although you do that, too), but also letting go for a short period of time. When you're working on something, you're focused. Your mind is concentrated and is making an effort. When you take a breather, you turn it loose so it can come and go as it pleases.

In practical terms, this amounts to distracting yourself. The best way to achieve this is by doing something that doesn't require you to think. For example, you could make a cup of tea, water the plants, wash the dishes, straighten up the living room, take out the garbage, run an errand or go for a short walk.

Between sessions, I often go for a walk around the block. It doesn't take longer than five minutes or so, but it makes for an excellent breather.

In all of the examples mentioned above, you get away from your desk and go do something. This is essential. Taking a breather while you're still at your desk isn't enough. As far as your mind is concerned, when you're surfing the internet or reading something on a

If you find yourself thinking "Hang in there!", take a short break

website your mind is still focused. It can't let go and so can't gain an overview.

Only when physical activity is part of your job – for example, if you're a gardener or a plumber – should you sit down when you take a breather. In these professions, your thoughts are already often free to wander when you're on the job.

A breather has a positive effect in three ways. The first one, which is also the first to emerge, is that you inadvertently evaluate the task you just completed. You suddenly realize you forgot to mention something important, or that the wording of a text wasn't right.

The second is that it allows you to relax for a bit. You've just done something that takes effort, and now your body and mind would like to rest. This takes some time, just like your computer needs time to shut down. After a breather, you should feel relaxed. If you still find yourself thinking about the previous activity, take a little more time.

The third thing that happens during a breather is that potential activities for after the breather come to mind. This doesn't require you to do anything special, because it happens all on its own. This is the natural result of giving your thoughts free rein, and shows once again how important it is that a breather should not involve any mental effort. We'll make use of this aspect in Instruction 7.

When should you take a breather?

There are two good reasons to take a breather. The first one is because you've finished a task. You've written up your notes or prepared for the meeting. You might not have finished the entire task yet, but you have completed a portion of it. You've made an outline of what you want to do, but haven't fleshed it out yet. You can round off this part for now.

The second good reason is that your body or mind is telling you that you've used up your energy. You have to develop a feel for this. We often tend to ignore or suppress these signals. Just a little bit longer, we think, then we'll be done. While in fact our body is crying out for a moment of rest.

Before reading on, make a list of the ways your body tells you it would like to have a moment of rest. Then compare your list with my own, which you'll find on the opposite page.

Your body might use the following signals to indicate it needs a short break:

- Your concentration wanes; you have trouble keeping your mind on the task at hand.
- You start making mistakes.
- You forget things.
- You lose your enthusiasm.
- You work more slowly.
- Your back or shoulders hurt.
- You're easily distracted; you start surfing the internet or working inefficiently.
- You think to yourself: "Hang in there, just a little bit longer and I'll be done."

I was recently at a meeting of the Buddhist Union of the Netherlands. There had already been two hours of intensive discussions, and everyone had taken part. "Shall we keep going for another hour?" asked the chairperson. "Then we'll be done. Or would you like to take a short break?" Even the Buddhists can err on this point! The truth is that taking a break allows you to pick up where you left off feeling refreshed. With no break, there's a good chance you'll find yourself in the middle of endless debates in which people are irritable and start to go off on tangents. In fact, taking a break saves time, even though it was not deliberately intended to do so. Having "no time" for a breather, therefore, is no excuse.

A time-out for yourself

There's another good time to take a breather: when you're not sure what to do. You're wavering between two options, or you're in doubt as to how you should answer an email. If you get up and get some fresh air and then go back to work, you'll be more likely to know which option to go for or how you want to reply.

Professions with few opportunities for breathers

There are, of course, professions where it's not possible to stop what you're doing when your body and mind start giving you the signals that indicate they are in need of rest. One example is teaching, and in my opinion it's one of the contributing factors to the high levels of absenteeism and burnout in this sector.

Teachers often have to teach classes back to back, with only occasional short breaks. During this time they have to prepare for the next class and are often approached by students and co-workers, which means there is no time for a breather even during their "break".

Even so, there are ways to work around this. The teacher can introduce some variations into the curriculum. He or she can alternate giving explanations (strenuous) with having students work silently on their own (restful) or with watching an informative or entertaining film as a class (restful and relaxing).

On her own initiative, an English teacher on one of my courses decided to start each of the classes she taught with a breather, which consisted of three minutes of silence. This had a beneficial effect on both the class and on her. She told me about the time she forgot about it, and the students asked for it themselves: they said they hadn't had their "meditative moment" yet.

Alternating between tasks and activities that require different kinds of energy is an important aspect of Time Surfing. When we start using the seventh and final instruction, "Use your intuition when choosing what to do", we'll notice that this kind of variation happens naturally.

In the beginning, it's good to make a conscious effort to create time for breathers. I know people whose tendency to keep going is so entrenched that they set an alarm on their phone to go off at specific intervals. Personally, I'm more of a believer in choosing a moment that feels natural – for example, when your attention wanes or when you're done with a certain part of a task. To practise this, you need to listen carefully to your body and enjoy getting away from your workplace for a while.

INSTRUCTION 4:

GIVE YOUR FULL ATTENTION TO DROP-INS, CREATING A RELATIONSHIP WITH EVERYTHING YOU WANT TO DO

Explanation

Give your full attention to interruptions that come between you and your main activity, whether it's a co-worker who wants to ask you a question or an incoming phone call.

By shifting the focus of your attention, you experience the interruption as a separate item rather than as a disruption, and don't stay suspended inbetween two things. It's also possible to give someone your undivided attention while telling them you don't have time right now. When the interruption has passed, you return fully to whatever you were doing previously.

At the same time, it is important to limit distracting drop-ins as much as possible. Every distraction also means you need to regain your concentration. You can find a private place to work, or let people know when you shouldn't be interrupted. Turn off pop-ups and notifications, and mute your phone when your attention is required.

A drop-in can also come in the form of a reminder: arriving while you're working and you suddenly think of something you'd like to do later. Give this one your full attention too, by briefly visualizing what you have to do to make this happen. Now you're inwardly prepared. Later on, your intuition will pick the right moment for you to carry out this activity. As a check, you can put this activity on a list or in your appointment calendar.

Do this with all of your tasks in both the near and distant future: create a relationship with them. Imagine yourself actually doing them, and think about anything you will need (tools, information, etc.) to complete the task. By picturing the activity in this way, you are letting your subconscious know about it, which means it will then work behind the scenes to help you get ready to implement it. Your agitation will also disappear as a result, because the task is already somewhat "in hand".

Example

You're discussing something with a client when a co-worker interrupts you: they need you to explain something to them before they can continue their work. You apologize to the client, and ask if he can wait for a moment. You calmly give your co-worker the information they need, and then turn back to the client. This way of dealing with an interruption is better than giving a hasty explanation to your co-worker while keeping some of your attention on your client.

You're giving a presentation to a small group when someone asks a question about a related, but not strictly relevant, subject. You stop what you're doing and direct all of your attention to this person. You say that you'll return to this question later. At the end of the presentation, you address the question. In this case, you don't address the question immediately because it's too far off the main topic. However, when you deliver this message, you do so with your full attention.

Telephone drop-ins

You're making dinner and your mother calls. You're flipping potatoes with one hand and holding the phone with the other as you listen to your mother. Your attention shifts from the fried potatoes to your mother's back problems. Turn down the heat under the potatoes. Give your mother your full attention as you tell her she's calling at an awkward moment, but that you can talk after dinner. Then go back to your cooking. After dinner, you call her back.

Drop-ins in the form of thoughts

As you're working, it occurs to you that you want to bring your camera to work tomorrow so that you can take a picture of the project you're working on. You visualize checking to see whether the camera is charged and putting it in your bag. Then you can make a note in your appointment calendar in the space for today's date.

A friend is celebrating her birthday on Saturday. You visualize picking out a gift, even though you don't yet know what that gift will be. Afterwards, you don't have to make a conscious effort to remember this.

Commentary

The term drop-in refers to someone or something that arrives unannounced. For our purposes, it might be a person who knocks on your office door and interrupts you while you're in the middle of something. They drop in with a question that may or may not be important. Or they just want you to hear a story about their weekend.

If you're concentrating on something and have, say, just come up with exactly the right wording for a sentence in a report you're writing, the appearance of this drop-in feels ill-timed to say the least. You desperately want to keep your focus and really resent the interruption. You secretly wish that the interrupter would hurry up and leave so you can get back to what you were doing.

At this moment, then, one part of you is with the task you were engaged with before the interruption and the other is with the drop-in itself and, as a result, you answer the question halfheartedly or reply with general irritation. This is unpleasant for both parties. You get tense and the other person doesn't feel heard. They might even stay longer and keep pressing their point, or come back later with yet another question.

You can observe this phenomenon clearly in young children. You're working on the computer when your son comes in to show you the spaceship he's just made. If you're preoccupied and tell him yes, it's very nice, but you don't want to be disturbed right now, he'll come back two minutes later and ask you to help him look for a part he needs. He doesn't just want you to say something about his creation, he wants your attention. He'll get this if you turn toward him, take his spaceship in your hands and really look at it. Then you can tell him you want to finish what you're doing first and that you'll come to find him in a bit. He'll respect this.

For both you and the other person, it's more relaxing and also more effective if you stop what you're doing when faced with a drop-in. Make a complete shift. Let go of your activity completely, give all of your attention to the drop-in and then return fully to what you were doing. See the interruption as a separate bead on your string of time.

In the meantime, you're free to choose whether to comply with the drop-in's request, agree to talk later or refer the drop-in to someone else.

Deal with telephone interruptions in the same way. If anything, the message here is even stronger: let go of your computer screen and be totally available for the conversation. The communication will be more satisfying for both parties if you're completely present.

What's remarkable is that the perfect wording you had in your head, or whatever it was you had finally alighted upon before you made the shift, is still right there after you finish talking with the drop-in. As soon as he's gone, you know where you left off and remember what it was you wanted to write.

Shift your attention fully

Drop-ins inside your head

In addition to external drop-ins in the form of people or phone calls, there are also internal drop-ins that come from our own minds and exist solely inside our heads. These are thoughts that are concerned with things that need to happen later. There are two different categories. I'll talk here about the things we shouldn't forget: those things we want to remember so we can do them in the near future. In the next instruction, the fifth, we'll talk about "gnawing rats" – that is, the things we put off.

The category that consists of those things we need to do in the near future and which send us messages in the form of thoughts is an important one, because these kinds of reminders are there with us all day, every day, and the form they take is always changing.

These thoughts could be reminding you to think of a birthday present to buy for a friend, fill in an evaluation form, make a grocery list for what you need for supper or email the link you promised to send to a co-worker.

Without realizing it, you usually reject these kinds of attention-grabbers in exactly the same way you tend to treat actual drop-ins. They show up when you're busy working, just when you're concentrating on something else. All of a sudden, there they are, with their foot in the door and demanding your attention.

They ask you to pay attention to them for a while but, as far as you're concerned, they're coming at a bad moment. If you don't respond and instead push away the thought (*I'll deal with that later*), it's still there in the background and will keep trying to get your attention.

Here, as well, give the drop-in your full attention. Turn toward it and look it straight in the eye. See what it needs and what you have to do to make this happen.

The best way to do this is to go one step further and visualize the activity. Imagine yourself walking into a store and picking out a gift. In your mind's eye, see yourself filling out the evaluation form and sending it in. In this way, you establish a relationship with the future activity, just as you would with a person. The thing you need to do knows it has been heard and settles down. The trust that has been created between you and your intuition makes sure that the task will be carried out. It won't bother you any more. You can trust your intuition to remember the activity. Taking this final step is important. The message has been sent and it's not necessary to keep checking to see whether that's still the case.

True calm arises only when you trust that creating a positive relationship with the activity is enough to remind you about it at the right moment later on.

Exercise

Envision the things you want to do today or tomorrow and visualize yourself doing them. then let it go.

Preferably, you visualize doing a task the moment the thought "arrives", or the first time you notice the drop-in. If you break something, visualize repairing or replacing it. When you suddenly remember that you have to get a new passport, visualize filling in the form and getting your photo taken.

Using a checklist

As you get to grips with Time Surfing, especially in the very beginning, you can use a checklist as an aid. On this list, you note down the things you shouldn't forget, but not when you will do them. You can look at this list later on to make sure you haven't missed anything. On it can be written things you have to do in the future, but which you need more time for or which require you to be creative or focused.

Look at the list as often as you like in the beginning, but train yourself to trust your intuition when it comes to doing them, as described in Instruction 7. If you come across an item on the list and think "this always seems to fall by the wayside", visualize it again and try to find out why it keeps escaping your attention.

Put the list away so that you have to open it or get it out in order to look at it. If it's always out in plain view, you may still feel pressured to check the list and start to plan. Leave the planning to your intuition.

An example of a checklist:

- buy lubricating oil to fix squeaky door
- call plumber
- buy gift for Sandra
- write song for anniversary

You'll notice that you will need this list less and less. The more you get used to creating positive relationships with your tasks, the more natural the system becomes. When things are quiet, you won't need a list at all. At such times, things get their turn as a matter of course.

A dispenser filled with surprise capsules

The principle of visualizing actions in the future, then letting them go and trusting they will get their turn, can be thought of in terms of those coin-operated dispensers filled with surprise capsules that children are so fond of. It's the surprise element that makes them so appealing – the child doesn't know exactly what the capsule will contain. Think of every task or job that presents itself to us and that we then visualize as being contained inside one of these capsules. So if we've visualized picking out a birthday gift for a friend, this action will end up inside the glass dispenser, just like all of the other future activities with which we've created a positive relationship. Into the dispenser also go the "gnawing rats" we befriend with the fifth instruction. A relationship has been created between them and your subconscious, and because of this they will now present themselves at the right time. When we talk about Instruction 7, it will become clear just how this dispenser works – which surprise capsule drops through the slot, and when.

Making it real

Whatever is in the dispenser is something that's become real for you. You might read a book review and think: "That book would make a nice gift for my friend." You'll also have a positive attitude toward the evaluation you have to complete, instead of thinking about these activities as yet more things that still have to be done. There will no longer be any pressure associated with them. By creating a relationship with a task you have to perform in the future, your system will register it as something positive and you'll be open to solutions.
If you don't do this, you might not even notice it when an opportunity arises. Then you'll probably complete the evaluation reluctantly and at the last minute.

Combining short tasks

You can combine short tasks that can be finished quickly or that you promised yourself you'd do today. Sending a file, rescheduling an appointment, checking to see that you have enough handouts for the talk tomorrow, sending a confirmation – these activities don't take much effort and can be dealt with as a single item, one after the other. It's best to jot down such jobs in your appointment calendar in the space provided for today's date. Some examples of this:

Our intuition notices only those things we've created a positive relationship with

- confirm restaurant booking
- email Andrew about extra key
- pocket money for kids
- send Carlos photo

You also do these short tasks when your intuition prompts you to, adding it to your string as a single bead, the bead of the "short tasks".

When drop-ins arrive together, give them deferred attention

Sometimes several drop-ins arrive at the same time. This can happen at work and is common in schools. At such times, you can give them "deferred attention". At the start of class or before a test, a number of students might come to the teacher with questions all at once. He will then have to give them deferred attention. He can say:

"I'll walk through the classroom shortly, and when I pass your desk you can ask me your question." Also here, the best way to get this message across is to look directly at the student who asked for help.

Jobs with lots of drop-ins

In some professions, the work consists mainly of dealing with drop-ins. My family doctor's waiting room is informal and homely. The desk of his assistant Ria is right in the middle of the room, and the patients are seated around her. You can hear her answering questions on the phone. You can see her printing out prescriptions and talking to patients. Every time I'm there, I'm filled with admiration at the way she approaches things. She seems to embody this instruction in everything she does. Again and again, she focuses her attention on one of the many people around her and their questions and, if there are children who need to be soothed, she gives them her undivided attention. She appears to be choosing her next action intuitively. Answering questions and getting things done are interspersed with conversation and humour.

Too many drop-ins

At the same time, it is important to deliberately limit the number of possible drop-ins so that you can only be interrupted by what is functional for you. Therefore, let people in your environment know when you're available for questions. You can make it harder for people to interrupt you by finding a quiet place to work, or by working from home on certain days. In open-plan offices, it can be helpful to wear noise-cancelling headphones. This will keep people from disturbing you for less important things. Team members can make a roster for answering the phone and decide on the best times for sharing information. Also, make sure you regain control of your phone and your PC. Turn off pop-ups and notifications as much as possible and mute your phone when your attention is required.

Lightening up

Giving your full attention to drop-ins is a simple instruction that immediately provides more calm. It's pleasurable to really take some time for a co-worker, a friend or your child, and then turn your full attention back to the task at hand. It's nice to know that the things you want to do in the future will no longer be buzzing around your head, but will instead calmly wait their turn.

INSTRUCTION 5:

BECOME AWARE OF "GNAWING RATS" AND TRANSFORM THEM INTO "WHITE SHEEP"

Explanation

Befriend your "gnawing rats" – the tasks that eat away at you under the surface, demanding your attention but not receiving it. Whatever it is that you're putting off, whether it's cleaning out the shed or filling in your tax return, you should go and visit it. Have an actual look at it if you can, or if not, then visualize it. Tell yourself you don't have to do the task right away. You're only going to get acquainted with it. You can then identify the reasons for your strained relationship with this task.

As you do this, answer the following questions:

- What do you know and what do you know how to do? How would you start?
- What don't you know? What's missing?

Do you first have to gain certain knowledge, or is there something you need help with? Are you apprehensive about something because it contains an element that makes you nervous? You can imagine watching a movie in which you perform the task, while at the same time feeling the tension that goes hand in hand with this for you.

By identifying where the problem lies, or by visualizing the step that's hard for you, you create a relationship with the task. Although it might not yet have become a deep friendship, it's become real for you, and because of this your mind will search for a solution. Leave it to your intuition to choose when to actually carry out the task.

Example

At work, there's a project you keep putting off. Even though it's important, you don't make a start. You don't quite know why.

Here, as well, in the process of befriending what we shall call this "gnawing rat", there are a number of steps involved as you turn toward the problem.

You ask a co-worker to be your sounding board and tell him about the project. You explain how you would like to go about it, and that you would like him to ask you questions about the various steps and what you might need. By examining things in this way, you also find out where your resistance lies.

What you discover is that you're going to have to work together on this project with someone you don't get on with very well. This person has openly criticized you on a number of occasions in the past, and has said that you're too pushy. The way you see it, this person can be chaotic, and this annoys you. By discussing the project with a neutral co-worker, you've brought the reason to the surface.

Now you can set about fixing the problem. You seek out the person in question and ask for his or her vision for the project and also for feedback on your approach. The conversation provides clarity for both parties, and trust is restored.

You've been finding water under the washing machine for the past week. Wiping it up provides only a temporary solution, and it quickly turns into a gnawing rat. Time to befriend it. In the following example, you'll see that this involves a number of steps that require you to assess the situation and then take action.

First, see if you can figure out where the water is coming from. You'll also need the washing machine's user manual (step 1). If you're organized, you'll find this in the binder where you keep all of your user manuals. Otherwise, you can probably download this from the internet.

Under "problems and solutions", you read that the filter might be blocked. You clean the filter. If the washing machine keeps leaking, you'll have to go further (step 2).

If you feel capable of doing so, you pull the washing machine away from the wall and open it up so you can find the leak. A hose might have worn out and become porous. If you find the faulty part, remove it. Where can you get a new hose (step 3)? You enter the serial number on the manufacturer's website and find the replacement part. You order the hose and replace it.

Another option is to call a plumber. But how will you find someone who's capable and not too expensive? You ask friends about their experiences or go on the internet yourself to find someone in your neighbourhood who's received good reviews.

Commentary

My daughter has pet rats. They're lovable, intelligent animals. Unfortunately, they don't live very long – around two years – and we've already held many funerals in the backyard. Everyone drops a flower or leaf into the little grave, and the children give a eulogy for "Kiwi", "Moon" or "Star".

"Mia" is our housemate right now and, because she's on her own, my wife leaves the cage door open so that she can interact freely with us. In the evening, when the house is quiet, she comes into the kitchen and steals dry cat food. She then goes and sits underneath the cupboard. Although we can't see her, we can certainly hear her chewing. Once she's stashed away enough of the cat food in her secret spots around the house, she'll come over and climb onto your foot and up the leg of your trousers. The journey ends on your shoulder. At night, Mia has to go back in her cage, otherwise we wake up in the middle of the night to the sounds of crunching and gnawing under our bed as Mia works on her hidden cat food.

A gnawing rat keeps you up at night. Things you put off can do this as well. When you put off certain important things, they start to gnaw at you and can even keep you from sleeping.

When we cover gnawing rats on my course, I have people make a list of things they regularly avoid doing and that subsequently eat away at them. Paperwork and tax returns score high, closely followed by redecorating, cleaning out cupboards and sheds, repairing the printer and sorting out for recycling those clothes you no longer wear.

When you think about your gnawing rats, you'll find there is often an obstacle that hides behind the thing that needs to be done. You don't have the right tools, for example. The user manual has to be around here somewhere, but where? Maybe it's that the shop that has the part is on the other side of town. Or it's going to be a lot of work. That cupboard or shed will take you at least one whole day, you think.

It's not so much a matter of getting the job done immediately as it is about being able to befriend it, and by doing so take the negative charge out of the situation.

One participant in a course had a gem of a gnawing rat. At the back of her yard was a mound of sand that was left over from the construction of her patio. It had been there for quite some time. She gradually found herself spending less and less time in this part of the garden, even though it was an otherwise beautiful spot, with fragrant rosebushes.

This is also a characteristic of gnawing rats – you unconsciously avoid them. I asked her what she needed in order to clear away the pile of sand. "A wheelbarrow," she said. "And I've actually got one, but it has a flat tyre …" This is a good example of a hidden obstacle. "What do you have to do to fix the tyre?" I asked. "I have to bring it to the bicycle store," she answered. "But I can't get it there on my own, and I can't get the wheel off because the bolts are rusted." Another obstacle. "You could oil it," another participant suggested. "Let's say that you're able to solve this problem," I said. "Where would you take the sand?" "I don't know," she said. "I wouldn't know what to do with it."

I told her there was nothing wrong with not knowing – all she needed to do was consciously realize that this was the case.

As I say, the secret to dealing with a gnawing rat is creating a relationship. This woman was avoiding the spot with the sand and so didn't have a positive, open relationship with it. But when you do create this relationship, it sets in motion the magical process that will lead to the solution.

The following week she came up to me and said: "The pile of sand is gone." "What did you do with it?" I asked. "I worked it into the garden," she told me. She'd talked about it with an acquaintance who was knowledgeable about gardening. From this person, she learned that a little sand in the soil of her garden wouldn't hurt it at all. The solution that presented itself turned out to be different from what she'd been expecting, and was actually closer to hand. But, to be able to see it, she first had to open a door – the inner door to the pile of sand. And you do this not by avoiding the spot, but by actually going there. This advice applies in general for the things you put off and which have become gnawing rats, and is something you can interpret literally where possible: go there.

Go and find your gnawing rats, create a relationship with them, and identify what you find difficult or what you're afraid of.

You don't have to know everything, but you do have to realize you don't know it

Take the example of a shed, attic or storage area. Over time, these places tend to become cluttered with all kinds of things. They're a mixed bag, and include a wide variety of items that we don't need right now but which might be useful in the future, or which have emotional value and so are hard to throw away.

This might be an old rusted bike, a tent that's still good but has been replaced by a more lightweight model, an air mattress with a puncture that still needs to be fixed or a painting your aunt gave you but that you don't really like.

The advice here is: go into the shed. Don't do anything yet, just look around. Observe and take stock. Make the space your own. And, just as with the pile of sand at the back of the yard, the first solutions will present themselves. A number of items will change hands and be donated to others. Other things will wait until that

Saturday afternoon when you say to yourself: "And now it's time to clean out the shed." You don't dread it any more but are actually looking forward to it.

A method for befriending gnawing rats

A good way to befriend gnawing rats of the "How do I do this?" variety is to talk about them. As you talk, you will naturally put your finger on the problem. But you can also analyse the situation on your own and figure out where the problem lies.

You can use the following method to deal with a gnawing rat. You can also approach a new task or assignment in this way, at the moment you're offered it. We'll take a closer look at this later on, when we talk about dealing with deadlines.

When analysing the situation, ask yourself the following four questions to help you befriend a gnawing rat:

1. **What do I already know? What do I know how to do? how can I get started?**
   - for the shed: Where can I put what?
   - for a problem: What do I already know about the solution?
   - for a new task: What do I already know I want to do?
2. **What don't I know? What knowledge do I lack? Which resources do I need to procure?**
3. **What do I need help with?**
4. **What am I apprehensive about?**

Finally, it can also be useful to examine if there are any "limiting beliefs" that paralyse you.

1. What do I already know? What do I know how to do? How can I get started?

Start with the bright side of the spectrum, where you're creative and take the initiative. It's important to identify what you already know or are able to do, because this helps you get started. Conversely, when you put things off, you'll actually forget to take note of this aspect.

When you embark on a project, you always know how you're going to do part of it, even though there might be a tricky element involved that you're not yet sure how to approach. Although you don't exactly know how to install a tap in the shower, you do know where to buy one and what kind you'd like to have. The painting from your aunt has mainly emotional value. What you do know is that you're not going to hang it up anywhere. What you don't know is what you're going to do with it.

2. What don't I know? What knowledge do I lack? Which resources do I need to procure?

After you've identified what you already know or know how to do, identify what you *don't* know or *don't* know how to do. If something's missing, this can lead to paralysis and cause you to keep putting off the task until later. Then you think, first I have to know this or get that or I won't be able to continue, but you don't take any steps to get it, because now you've made it into a big thing. If you learn to look directly at whatever it is you're missing, it will become real to your subconscious, as we've already seen. Now your mind will go looking for a solution on its own, like a plant goes toward the light. There's a good chance that before long you'll find something that will help you on your way. Or you'll meet someone who'll help you get closer to the solution.

You find the instructions for installing the tap at the home improvement store that sells it, and they'll also be there in the box it comes in. You take out the painting and look at it. Your aunt doesn't want it back. As you're looking at it, an idea comes to you. You get your camera and take a picture of it. You decide to sell it at a friend's garage sale so it can find a new owner. You give your old bike to your friend's son, who needs one and knows how to fix it up.

3. What do I need help with?

You can't bring that heavy sofa out to the kerb on your own. Learning to use a new computer program is easier and more fun if you do it with someone who already knows how to use it and can show you the basics.

Having to ask for assistance can also get in the way of performing a task. Not everyone finds it easy to ask for help. At such times, you might tell yourself that you don't want to bother anyone and try to do it on your own. However, because you barely make progress, it remains difficult and becomes a gnawing rat.

Actually, the truth is often quite the opposite. Instead of being "bothered" by your request, most people actually like helping others. Your friend's partner would be happy to help you learn the ins and outs of a number of Excel formulas. Your friends would be glad to come for an afternoon and help you move or redecorate. Of course, you can also hire people to help you with these things. With an accountant, you can finalize your bookkeeping for the year in a way that's both efficient and pleasant. My experience with my accountant Carla has shown me that this usually saves more time and worry than it costs in financial terms.

4. What am I apprehensive about?

This is an element that can lurk imperceptibly beneath the things you don't get around to doing. There is something about the task or its implementation that you're afraid of. It can be fear of rejection or criticism, or fear of being reproached for being out of touch for so long. Maybe you're afraid your decision will hurt the other person's feelings. Maybe you're apprehensive about something because there's a lot to do or because it will be difficult.

It's important to identify the presence of such emotional obstacles. With these kinds of feelings, we have the strong tendency to turn away from what we fear. We look for excuses so we don't have to do them.

We don't call the family member because we don't have time for such a long conversation. We don't join a co-worker at his table because he never listens to other people. We don't tell our neighbour that his Sunday morning DIY sessions are starting to get too loud because, if we do, he'll fly off the handle.

Here, as well, the advice is to turn toward this anxiety. Do this in your mind first of all. Imagine calling your family member, feel the tension and proactively formulate what you'd like to say. In your mind's eye, go and sit at your co-worker's table, start a conversation and watch a mutual interest emerge. In your mind, choose the approach

79

and phrasing you can use to tell your neighbour what's bothering you without blaming him.

While you allow the experience to wash through you, you might also feel nervous or anxious. By feeling this in advance and experiencing the emotions, you'll also be able to deal with them during the actual situation when the time comes. Here, as well, the key to the breakthrough is your openness, just as it is for the other aspects of a gnawing rat. Although you'll still feel nervous at the start of the conversation or encounter, it will gradually lessen and you'll be able to steer whatever happens next in the right direction.

When we cover the sixth instruction on "background programs", we will delve more deeply into dealing with emotional tension.

Limiting beliefs

There can be yet another reason for putting things off. You can be held back by what are known as "limiting beliefs". For example, you might think, "I've got to do it on my own," "It has to be perfect," or "Once I start, I want to keep going until I'm done."

In such cases, it's good to put the desired belief into words. This can be in the form of sentences like "I can ask for help," "Good is good enough," or "I can break it down into different steps." Sometimes it helps to just make a start, even if it's only for ten minutes. This gets you off on the right track and makes it easier for you to pick it up again later on.

Assignment

Make a list of your own gnawing rats. Choose one of them and analyse it using the four questions above. or talk about it with your partner or a friend. Ask this person not to offer their own solutions, but to ask questions. In the near future, take the time to befriend all of your gnawing rats, one by one.

White sheep

You might be surprised to find that you're not being asked to immediately do whatever it is that's gnawing at you. The assignment is only to establish a relationship with it. You let all of the various facets sink in and then let them go again.

The rat no longer gnaws at you and has settled down. It's no longer trying to get your attention but follows quietly behind. It now has white legs and a curly fleece – it's turned into a white sheep.

A gnawing rat is troublesome and keeps you awake at night. A white sheep is a very different animal. It's part of a flock, and the flock follows meekly behind the shepherd. The sheep symbolize the tasks that you plan to do in the future. When you become friends with them, they'll follow you loyally and won't get in your way.

By doing this, you give them the chance to present themselves at the right moment. This will be when you're in the mood for it. For example, when you're in the right frame of mind to write a text, repair something, make a request or work on your bookkeeping. You can read about how this works in Instruction 7.

Give special attention to what is positive and pleasant

In a certain sense, that which applies to what we put off also applies to those enjoyable and pleasant things that we unfortunately no longer get around to doing. The former involves things we don't feel like doing, the latter involves those things we really do want to do, but which gradually fall away because of the hectic nature of our lives.

The busier we are, the more we tend to sacrifice the things that are enjoyable. After all, they're not really urgent, and so end up at the back of the line. The longer the line, the longer whatever is at the back of the line has to wait, until its turn might never come. You will notice how during busy periods you sacrifice more and more pleasurable moments.

If you're a freelancer or have a demanding job in a company or organization, this kind of busyness has probably become the order of the day. In that case, you might do some work in the evening after dinner. On Saturday, you do the paperwork you didn't get to during the week. Although you see your family, you're unavailable.

You no longer have the time to read a good book. Your interests and passions aren't as keen as they once were. Things that take a bit more time – like keeping up with and expanding your music collection – fall away. You no longer have time to bake a cake or make a more complicated dish for dinner. You don't get around to cultivating your spiritual side or playing sports.

It's both unfortunate and unwise to go down this path. You're sacrificing the richness life has to offer, the things that give it colour. That which seems to be the outermost layer actually forms the foundation for happiness.

When your free time gradually becomes filled up, you can respond to this by consciously choosing to work less in order to create more breathing room. You give up some of your ambitions and income and get life in return.

Visualize what you enjoy but never get around to doing

But what is especially important is that you see the value of having time for your friends, your family and yourself, and focus attention on this as well. This is why I recommend that you actively place those things you long for most deeply in among the flock of white sheep.

The way to do this is the same as for drop-ins and gnawing rats. We can maintain our relationship with what we enjoy by imagining ourselves doing it, as well as how we're going to do it, including any steps along the way.

Say that you'd really like to see a dance performance again. You see yourself sitting in the hall watching a performance together with someone who shares your interest. You also remember a similar moment from the past that you also enjoyed. Notice how good this feels.

Meanwhile, nothing has actually happened. Nor does this mean it has to happen in the near future. But it has arrived as an option in the intuition's field of awareness, so that, when the time is right, this plan can bring itself to fruition.

Assignment

- *Think of the things you would enjoy doing but don't get around to.*
- *Choose one of them and imagine yourself doing it.*
- *Notice how glad it makes you feel. Then let it go again.*
- *Do this with all of the things you would like to do.*
- *Make this into a habit.*

INSTRUCTION 6:

OBSERVE BACKGROUND PROGRAMS

Explanation

Background programs keep pulling your attention away from what you're doing, and take it off to an agitated place somewhere inside your brain. It's as if you first have to restore order there before you can focus fully on your work.

This turbulence can take various forms: you're worried about your health, you're involved in a conflict with a co-worker, you've had a setback or your boss doesn't value your work enough.

These kinds of situations can cause a special and curious phenomenon in your mind: you start to fret. Your thoughts run in circles, looping around and around, getting no closer to a solution. Whether we try to restore a sense of calm by thinking about what caused it or by ignoring it with all our might, it doesn't help and keeps distracting us.

The secret here is that an emotional response is taking place beneath the surface, and this first wants to be felt. Only when this has been given the attention it needs and things have settled down will you be able to make the right decision or find the most appropriate approach.

Example

You have to go to the hospital for some tests. Every time you think about it, you get a knot in your stomach and a lump in your throat. You can reason with yourself that you won't feel much because of the sedative they'll give you, that the procedure is very short and that the nurses are friendly. None of this makes you any less nervous, though. What do you do with your fear?

The following option is a good one: go for a long walk. As you're walking, focus your attention on the feeling of fear in your body. Even though your thoughts keep floating back to the examination room, during your walk you focus your attention on how you physically experience your nervousness. Stress occurs when you resist this emotion. By feeling it, it will gradually subside on its own. It will then be easier for you to see the procedure in the proper light.

You're going to take a trip soon and, as it gets closer, you start to get nervous. You try to get this under control by writing down everything you still have to do, but your nerves keep playing up. Your nervousness doesn't have as much to do with the fact that you might forget something as it does with leaving the familiar behind and heading for the unknown.

Do the following: sit down and close your eyes. Take the time to feel your nervousness. Focus your attention on your breathing. Allow the feeling to be present in your body and to fade away on its own. Take whatever time you need for this.

You get an email from a co-worker, which everyone on the team is copied into, to remind you that you still haven't done a certain task. Although it's true, there were other things going on at the time that were much more important and took priority. This really irritates you, or makes you angry. You keep thinking about this person and the wording you will use to put him in his place.

Take the time to feel this emotional response and to let it subside on its own using one of the two ways explained in the previous examples. When you've calmed down, seek out the co-worker and tell him why your priorities changed. Also tell him you would prefer it if he spoke to you directly in future, and that involving the rest of the team wasn't necessary.

Commentary

A while back we had some aggravation in our house. Our 12-year-old son had gradually claimed my wife's laptop for his own use and had been extremely creative in installing all kinds of programs that made this laptop more attractive or user-friendly.

He would proudly show us his latest acquisition and said we should download all of this great stuff too. But the side effect of this was that the laptop became slower and slower and more badly behaved. Our son got impatient and angry. With all of these headaches, he decided we needed a new laptop. That old thing was worthless, anyway.

Instead of buying a new one, however, we decided to try a drastic form of treatment for the laptop: first a backup and then a complete reinstallation. Now it runs just as smoothly as it did when it was brand new. Clearly, the laptop had just become clogged by all of the background programs that had been installed on it.

We humans also have programs that run behind the scenes. And they also slow us down. We can be doing our work (our main program) and be thinking about our relationship in the back of our mind (the background program). Again and again, our thoughts drift back to last night's argument.

Or it could be we've had a pain somewhere in our body for a while now. What could that mean? It couldn't be anything serious, could it? Maybe it's finally time to have it looked at. While we're trying to work, our mind is preoccupied with what's bothering us. It does its best to consider the situation from all sides. And it encourages us, or comes up with scenarios it thinks would allow us to get the situation under control again.

The only thing is … it doesn't work. We just keep brooding, going over it again and again like a fly that wants to be outside but keeps bumping into the window.

Two systems

We have two systems inside us that we humans use to respond to what happens around us. One is the cognitive system – our intellect; the other our emotional system – our feelings.

Often, both systems are at work simultaneously. For example, when we get frightened by a dangerous passing manoeuvre of a fellow road-user and we reflect on what happened. Or when we like how something tastes and try to name what's in it.

Our emotional system is much older than our intellect. We share the former with the higher mammals; being able to use feelings to respond was an important step in our evolution. This development meant that mammals could then go looking specifically for that which was pleasant or tasty and try to avoid those things that were unpleasant or dangerous. The intellect evolved much later, as part of the development of language in humans. When you think, you're in fact talking to yourself. It was a new step in evolution, and made it possible for humans to be more detached when responding to events and feelings.

Thinking allows us to compare a particular situation with other experiences and things we learned earlier, and to adapt our emotional response accordingly. Examples of such symbiotic reasoning would be: *Although I can feel my fear of heights, I know I can't fall from here*, or *If I can manage to stay calm when parenting my children, I will be much more effective than if I show my frustration.*

So far, so good. However, as well as working together harmoniously, the two systems can also work against each other. This is because each of the systems has its own conditions. An emotion, first and foremost, wants to be felt. The intellect, meanwhile, wants to understand things and reach logical conclusions. Our mind interprets emotions like fear, pain and sadness as distressing and arrives at the logical conclusion that, because of this, feeling such negative emotions must be avoided. This causes the emotional system to short-circuit.

Let's take the example of suddenly finding yourself in a traffic jam. For lots of people, this no longer evokes an emotional response. It happens so often that they've gotten used to it. But I well remember the insight a traffic jam gave me into how emotions work. The same thing can happen when the bus or train you're waiting for doesn't come, or when the bridge opens and a boat glides by at a speed that strikes you as belonging to another time.

It happened at the start of my research on stress. On that particular occasion, I was in the car on my way to a potential new client, the head of the human resources department in a hospital. I wasn't used to the morning *An emotion* rush hour and all of the cars that *wants to be felt* quickly jammed the roads. I was halfway there when things started to slow, and 30 seconds later I found myself in a traffic jam. I was very annoyed, because I considered this to be an important meeting, and didn't want to be late. I started to get irritated by how slowly the traffic was moving and by the way the car in front of me would slowly accelerate and then brake.

I felt my throat squeeze shut and my heart beat faster. I had the telephone number of my client written down in my appointment calendar but not in my phone, so I couldn't call to let him know I was running late. I glanced at the clock and saw the precious minutes ticking away. My thoughts got the upper hand: Why doesn't that man in front of me step on the gas? When I get there, there won't be enough time left to talk about everything. I might as well turn around at the next exit …

I didn't want to be late, which of course was going to happen. I didn't want to have to explain what had happened only to hear that, unfortunately, there wasn't enough time left for our talk, which would probably also happen. I didn't want any part of this extremely annoying situation.

Then I told myself that I shouldn't make things so complicated. After all, it wasn't the end of the world.

There was nothing more I could do about it now – I just had to accept it and see how things went.

But this line of reasoning didn't help me calm down. I was still steamed up. Apparently, accepting the situation required more than just using sound reasoning. Then I focused my attention on how it felt. I noticed how I clenched the steering wheel. How tensed my body was, all the way up to my shoulders. I tried to release the tension, which only worked to a certain extent. My breathing was shallow and my chest felt tight. Sitting in this traffic jam gave me plenty of time to observe what my body was doing. In the process, I noticed that by focusing my attention on my feelings, the tension became less. After a while, I started to breathe more freely and more deeply. And, to my amazement, I observed that I was calming down, and had started to accept that I was going to be late.

The purpose of emotions

Although the mind may see emotions that cause the body to go on the alert as problematic, they are in fact extremely useful.

First of all, they warn us that something is wrong and that we have to take action. Pain is useful because it acts as an alarm. Fear also functions as a warning sign. Take a fear of heights. It warns you to be careful when you're walking along that narrow mountain path. You'll also feel your inner alarm go off when you're out skating and hear the ice beneath you start to crack.

Second, the emotion makes sure the body is in an optimal condition to respond. Vital body functions are at the ready when a critical situation arises. You're alert, and out of the corners of your eyes you can see everything that's going on around you – in a fraction of a second, you've managed to catch that falling teacup.

And third, they have another wonderful quality, one that falls into our lap like an unexpected reward: the emotion we just felt allows us to process whatever caused it!

This is what happened when I let go of the unnecessary tension and stopped resisting the anxiety that was there in my body. The feeling subsided, and I was able to accept that I was going to be late.

This last phenomenon applies in general to emotional situations. You can come to terms with the fact that you were in a precarious situation when you allow yourself to feel the fear that accompanied this. You can calm down after being treated unfairly if you allow the emotional pain it caused to be present.

Emotions allow us to integrate and come to terms with what happened

This also applies to intensely emotional situations. Grieving means having the courage to feel a loss, which makes it possible to integrate and come to terms with it. It allows the sorrow to dissipate over time.

We'll now take a closer look at two major kinds of background programs.

Worry

The things we worry about are an important source of background programs. We might worry about money, our job, our health or the health of others or our children.

93

Worrying comes from uncertainty, because we don't know what the future will bring, and is in fact a form of fear. In critical situations, the thought machine inside our head runs at full speed. We try to analyse how things could have reached this point, and envision scenarios of everything that could possibly happen. Our mind tries to think its way through the situation until things settle down.

But that doesn't happen. Things don't settle down by thinking about them. While of course it's good to examine how realistic your worries are, there's an additional step you need to take to be able to come to terms with them.

Here as well, the emotion wants to be felt. Worry is fear, and, as we've already seen, one of the functions of fear is to serve as a warning signal – it indicates there is danger present. The only way our system can tell we've understood the warning signal is when the feeling has been accepted and felt. When we ignore it, the alarm can't be turned off. After all, it's there to help us and watch over us. Struggling to control the situation hides what we're actually doing: rejecting our feelings.

You could be worrying about your parents' health, your financial situation or your children's future. The emotion provides you with an unpleasant feeling of tightness. In fact, it tells you in its simple language nothing more than: "take care". Accepting these situations, rather than stifling them, means that you befriend your worries, just like your gnawing rats.

Paradoxically, the right thing to do when we worry is to feel your uncertainty, feel your fear. Feel its physical presence in your body and give it space. Once you've felt it, its force will diminish, the same way the wind dies down after a storm. You'll become calm and start to think clearly.

Now you'll see the situation in an impartial and realistic way. The imaginary doomsday scenarios are gone.

Once the fear has faded, you can start to let in trust. This is one of the most profound things a person can do for themselves: trust. Trust that you will find the way and that you can develop an intimate relationship with this path, now, later and always. You can let your plans emerge from this feeling. The ideas will be practical and appropriate. They won't be fed by fear. They'll arise from a sense of calm about the situation.

Feeling hurt

A co-worker makes a hateful remark. You ask for something that's important to you and get a blunt response. Your intention is misunderstood. Hurt feelings can produce a powerful emotional reaction, similar to pain. As a result, we also contract physically.

Here as well, we usually inwardly reject the situation. We wish it hadn't happened. We have a lot of resistance, and want to fix it as soon as possible. We want to make the other person see reason or we want revenge, and look feverishly for the best way to achieve this. All kinds of outcomes go through our head.

To be able to respond well when you feel hurt, it's important to become calm first. And in most cases, the best course of action is to respond. By seeking out the other person and talking about how you feel, you can clear up any misunderstandings or come to understand the other's different point of view or approach.

If you respond while tensions are still running high, there's a good chance the situation will escalate.

Clarity and calm about the situation are only possible once the emotional response has been felt and has subsequently *Respond only once you've calmed down* subsided. This means that you have to feel the pain, even though you might secretly wish it on the other person.

You also have to be willing to see the situation from the other person's point of view. And you have to get the other person to do the same for you by describing how they think you experience things.

Integration

When we're in situations we find intense, our system of logical thought and comprehension can easily become entangled with our underlying emotional system. To untangle the knot – or, better yet, to keep this knot from forming – it's important to proceed in the right order when integrating something that's happened.

The proper sequence is to feel first and think second, instead of the other way around. First we have to experience the emotion and, in the calm and clarity that then ensues, we can consider which steps to take. During this feeling process, our thoughts will keep trying to elbow their way to the front and take charge.

They're not going to let themselves be sidelined so easily! It's futile to try to push away your thoughts. Just like when you press your hand over a jet of water in a fountain and the other jets flow with greater force, your scorned thoughts will only come back with a vengeance.

Another possibility is to observe thoughts rather than follow them. This happens to be precisely what you do, and practise doing, when you meditate. The thoughts are there, but you don't lay claim to them. Their presence is accepted, but you don't identify with them.

If you want to watch your thoughts and not be drawn into their endless constructions, you'll need to create a separate time for this. If you're in the middle of work, or if there are other people around and you might get distracted, this can keep you from staying with your feelings at that moment. The best thing to do then is to take a short break. Taking a brisk walk is ideal. You're away from it all, you're breathing more deeply because you're physically active and you're able to really feel the emotional response.

Another good option is to find a quiet place where you won't be disturbed so you can be by yourself for a while. If you have experience with meditation, you could do so now.

Just as in the example of the traffic jam, try to release the tension in your muscles. You can't let go of the emotion itself, which we can imagine as the crest of a wave, but you can help to smooth the waters around it. Tell yourself that this feeling doesn't have to go away. The emotion can ebb away on its own without our will becoming involved. If we were to use willpower – for example, by trying to "breathe through" the emotion – we would come face to face with how little power we have in this area. The emotion interprets this attempt, like a child who is ignored and then screams for attention, as: "The body doesn't want to feel me, so I have to do everything I can to be felt." This results in even more tension.

In both cases, whether walking or sitting still, you focus your attention on the physical sensations. Commit yourself to a certain amount of time for this. This is important, because during the entire process you'll continue to feel resistance, and this can translate into thoughts that will try to get you to stop.

Be patient and keep returning to observing things in an open and relaxed way. Allow the thoughts to arise and present their arguments, but as soon as you notice you're in the middle of something your mind has constructed, let it go and return to what you're feeling. Do this faithfully for the whole time you committed to beforehand.

The cycle of an active integration process consists of four recurring elements:

You feel the emotion – an argument arises – you notice this – and let it go – you return to feeling the emotion – a new argument arises – you notice this – and let it go – you return to feeling the emotion, and so on.

If the moment doesn't lend itself to going off on your own, you can also allow the emotion to resurface later on. Once you're alone, your thoughts *It's never too late to integrate* will return to the incident and you'll be able to feel the emotion again. This is also a good moment to use one of the approaches mentioned above.

Now the worries in your head have come to rest and you face all tasks and projects you intend to do in the future with an open mind, it's time to leave the coast, paddle toward the waves and start Time Surfing.

USE YOUR INTUITION WHEN CHOOSING WHAT TO DO

Explanation

Your intuition can manage your time much more effectively than your mind. It takes more factors into account and is also more flexible.

When you're focused on what you want to do right now, rather than on checking items off a list, this creates calm. Using your intuition to make choices also means you do things at the "right" time and, as a result, you're always fuelled by inspiration.

You choose what you're going to do during a breather. At that moment you're doing something that doesn't require any mental effort, which creates an inner state that allows the intuition to do its job. Suitable options will arise on their own and you'll know what to do next. The more you trust your intuition to be a good manager, the better it will work.

Example

You get to work and make a cup of tea or coffee. The day before, you already had a look at your appointment calendar. You know which appointments you have today and this week, and also the hours you have open. You have an overview of your schedule for the coming weeks. You know what has to be done, and when.

During the first few minutes – which actually function as a breather – you decide to do task A. Often it's a good idea to rein in your curiosity and the inclination to open your email straight away. After around 40 minutes, you come up against a problem you're not able to figure out immediately. You put aside task A for the time being, get up and take a breather. During the breather, the solution to the problem suddenly occurs to you.

You go back and pick up task A where you left off. Over the next 30 minutes, you're able to bring this to a satisfying conclusion and save your work. Now is occurs to you that you want to send a certain email and to answer another one you left "simmering" yesterday. You open your email program, proceed to these two messages and then read the new emails in your inbox. You answer some messages and consciously let others continue to "simmer", closing your email program. Then you take another breather. During the breather, you think of something you want to add to task A. You make a note of this, but don't flesh it out yet. Now your intuition tells you that you can go on to task B, which is less demanding. Task B could be something that doesn't take much energy, like entering information into an Excel spreadsheet. During the breather you take after finishing task B, you get the urge to take on task C, a tricky job that will require you to concentrate fully. Task A presents itself again the following day, and you develop the additional material.

Commentary

"Use your intuition when choosing what to do" is the seventh and final instruction. In addition to having their own merits, the other instructions make this instruction possible. You can now rely on your intuitive radar when you go Time Surfing. This is incredibly liberating. Instead of constantly trying to piece together the problematic puzzle of time, your intuition will now do this for you, and do it with ease.

It knows how to navigate perfectly between all your tasks, between priorities and secondary activities, between the tasks that are recurring and those for which you've made delivery agreements. It doesn't balk at unforeseen urgencies because it has no set plan.

It presents not only the essential tasks, but also the useful and enjoyable ones. It provides for variety, because it chooses what fits the moment. It takes care of your work and also takes care of you, so that you continue to enjoy what you're doing and can comfortably keep up with the pace. By keeping your intuition as your guide, you regain mastery over time again!

How do you choose by intuition?

Most people already choose spontaneously to some degree during their free time. If you haven't made any plans, on Saturday your intuition will come up with good suggestions and in the right order! It will suggest that you change the burned-out light bulb, do some cleaning, read the article a friend gave you, cook a meal with your children and so on. It will also alternate between strenuous and relaxing activities with discernment. The less "enjoyable" necessary tasks will also get their turn.

To enable your intuition to do its job well, it's important not to focus and instead allow your thoughts to roam free. Only then can your intuition make associations using all of *Your intuition can manage your time more effectively than your mind* the information it has at its disposal and effortlessly put forward the best option for right now. During a breather, your mind is out of gear: you're doing something physical, such as making a cup of tea or taking a short walk, that doesn't require you to think. Our thoughts wander, and in so doing put the wonder of intuition to work: during a breather, it unconsciously selects one or more activities that you could do now. They occur to you spontaneously. From these activities, you choose the one that seems best to you. This means that breathers are absolutely essential to the instruction "Use your intuition when choosing what to do".

Our intuition usually presents us with a number of possibilities. They are all in harmony with the wavelength of the present moment. You consciously choose one of them. The others will probably get their turn later on. But this isn't a given, because in the meantime the wavelength may have changed.

Which factors does the intuition take into account?

The intuition takes the following factors into account:

- Everything that's been entered into your appointment calendar. This way, it's also aware of the time that's still available.

- All future tasks you've established a relationship with by assimilating or visualizing them.
- The gnawing rats you've befriended.
- Delivery agreements: Things you've agreed to finish by a certain date and which you've subsequently written down in your appointment calendar.
- Hidden delivery agreements: The preparations for a delivery agreement that have to be completed at an earlier stage.
- Your current energy level. Are you feeling rested and in good spirits? Are you feeling tired and has a task made your eyes glaze over? If the latter is true, your intuition will probably suggest a change of pace.
- The atmosphere you find yourself in. Is it quiet or noisy?
- The energy level of the people you work with.

And, finally, your intuition is exceptionally good at responding to any unexpected, special tasks that might come up. Because the choice it makes does not come through the conscious mind, whatever it chooses does not arrive as a result of painstaking deliberation but is there in a flash.

It's like the analogy of the glass dispenser filled with surprise capsules. Everything – including all of your work activities, odd jobs, phone calls to be made, reading to be done, cleaning and filing activities and staying in touch with friends – has ended up inside the dispenser as options. When you take a breather, your intuition turns the crank beneath the glass globe and one or more of the capsules falls through the slot. Expectantly, you open the capsule and are amazed to find that the contents fit this moment perfectly.

What's not in the dispenser can never fall through the slot! Your intuition won't be able to suggest as an option things you have a negative relationship with – that you're not open to. If you notice that a certain task never presents itself, take the time to visualize it again, and include all of its aspects.

Variety

An important difference with your old way of working is that during every new breather you can decide to do something else or to keep doing the same thing. Shorter jobs will allow themselves to be tucked inbetween sections of a larger one. You'll no longer spend half of the day slogging away on a text you just can't get to flow. All of the variety is the very thing that will ensure that later on there'll come a moment when you will be in the right mood for the text. The funny thing is, what your intuition chooses to do can sometimes surprise even you.

The right moment

The capsule that drops through the slot fits the present moment perfectly. Choosing with your intuition yields valuable returns. Your intuitive radar points out the activities that fit this exact moment in time. It takes into account how urgent something is, how you're feeling and what you just did, and chooses the best activity. As a result, you'll experience the proposed activity as the right one every time.

If it's a task that requires creativity, vision or clarity, you'll be inspired to do them. This will also have an effect on your state of mind during appointments and meetings that are already scheduled. The activities that surround them will take into account the energy the meeting will require. When you listen to your intuition, you're much more efficient than when you use willpower!

As a rule, efficiency is associated with doing your very best, knowing how to set priorities, not getting sidetracked and being focused. In practice, increasing efficiency can mean that an employee is required to fill in time sheets and determine whether the targets have been reached. Companies want their employees to work more effectively, and they also want to be able to assess this. Employees, though, usually experience this kind of monitoring as pressure and find it bothersome. But when you use the Time Surfing method, efficiency falls into your lap like ripe fruit. Without excessive exertion, without sweat and without outside pressure. You're always inspired, whether you're working out the details of a new assignment, having a conversation or filing documents.

Calm

The focus of Time Surfing is different. When you organize things in the usual way – identifying what needs to be done, setting goals and categorizing the activities – you constantly see what you still have to do. And this causes tension. When you use your intuition to navigate, you don't see everything all of the time, but you don't need to, either. It's already been filed away in your subconscious because you received it at the start with an open mind and have visualized the tricky bits.

Your intuition is free to juggle all of the items and drop them into your schedule at just the right moment without you needing to know which criteria it used for this. It's enough to trust. And the more you are able to trust, the more calm you will experience. Trust is actually synonymous with calm.

During our vacations, my father would sometimes take a scenic mountain road. My mother, who tends to be anxious, would close her eyes. To our delight, she'd cry out "Oh, Marcel, no!" at every curve. Even now when we drive home after visiting them in their senior housing community, she'll be uneasy until I call to let her know we got home safely. Worry, no matter how well intentioned, brings stress. And trust brings calm.

Both at home and at work

Spontaneously choosing what you're going to do works just as well at home as it does at work. Nowadays it's often possible to do some of your work from home, and you can easily alternate between your work activities and your personal activities. Loading the washing machine is a good way to take a breather.

Straightening up the house and cleaning are tasks that leave you feeling refreshed after a period of intense concentration.

Avoid using dual controls

Making the transition from control to trust requires some patience and a light touch. We're so conditioned and have become so used to trying to use *Do things at the* our head to monitor things and *right moment* be in control that we think we have to keep doing this when we navigate using trust. In other words, we use dual controls.

This is what that looks like in practice: Although you consistently use your intuition to choose what you're going to do, at the same time your mind thinks: "I hope I don't forget anything. I hope I finish it on time." As a result, you still feel agitated. When these things keep presenting themselves needlessly, go ahead and visualize them one more time and let them go again. You treat this as you would a child who can't fall asleep, patiently reassuring them whenever the need arises. Do this without exerting any pressure, because that will be counterproductive. After a while, your internal system will have become comfortable with the idea that it really can trust your intuition and the additional monitoring will fall away.

PART III: APPLICATIONS AND TOOLS
DEADLINES

We're so used to the word "deadline" that we no longer hear what it conveys. But, if we look more closely, the real meaning of the term is a surprising one. The word actually refers to a line that prisoners in the American Civil War were forbidden to pass. A deadline elicits in us an old animal reflex. When we cross the line from safety to a situation where our life is in danger, we respond like every other mammal. The function of this behaviour is to give us a chance at survival in extreme circumstances. You're calmly picking blackberries when suddenly a hungry wolf appears from behind the bush. Without a moment's hesitation, you climb the closest tree and swing from branch to branch to somewhere safer. You're driving on the highway and drumming on the steering wheel to the beat of the music on the radio. Then, out of the corner of your eye, you notice that the car merging into your lane from the right is moving far too slowly. You don't know how you do it, but in a split second you somehow manage to look in the rearview mirror, swerve sharply to the left and hold out your right arm to protect the person in the passenger seat. You barely miss the car as you shoot past and, looking at the elderly driver, you can tell he's entirely oblivious to his narrow escape.

You agree that you'll turn in the article next Friday. That's a long way off, and there's no need to start on it yet. Besides, there are a lot of other important things in your calendar right now, so you focus on them first. A week passes in this way.

Then it's Monday of the following week. That's not a good day for inspiration, and nor do you much feel like it on Tuesday either. On Wednesday you've got that big meeting. Thursday ... Right, now those ideas *Trust* really have to start to flow – but nothing *brings* happens. You dawdle around and don't get *calm* anything done. Friday ... This is it. You stall for a while. Then you snap at everyone and tell them you want to be left in peace. You sit down at your desk, and all of a sudden you know what you're going to write. You're on a roll, and knock out the entire story in just two hours.

There's not enough time to edit it thoroughly, but it's an inspired text.

You go into the weekend feeling satisfied, but then you notice you've used up all of your energy and don't feel like doing anything at all.

The fact is, using this survival mechanism comes at a price. It's as if you've had a bonfire and used up a week's supply of firewood in a single go. Your body then switches off so it can recharge.

The risks associated with frequent stress

It's not so bad when you use this mechanism once in a while. But when I ask about this during a course or a talk, there are always people who say they use this mechanism on a regular basis. There are even those who claim they can't get anything done without it, as if the stress of a deadline is essential to their performance. They will tell you: "I'm a last-minute man. I'm at my most creative when I run out of time."

This approach is nothing more than a story – an old, deeply ingrained habit. There really is another, more energy-efficient way.

For our body, frequent stress is a matter of simple arithmetic: it adds up. But it only presents you with the total bill once it's too late to turn things around.

Stress involves numerous bodily processes. This is logical, because they make sure our body is alert and ready to respond. The heart rate increases and our blood pressure goes up. This activates your sympathetic nervous system, which functions as the body's accelerator. The hormones adrenaline and cortisol are pumped into the blood and emit signals all over the body. Other processes, such as digestion and the sex drive, slow down to conserve energy. It also compromises the body's overall immune system.

When things have calmed down again, the process takes place in reverse order. However, it takes quite some time for these hormones to leave the body completely. If we dip into these reserves again before this process is completed, we elevate the hormone levels in our blood. And so it goes. Three steps up, two steps down. And then another three up, and only two steps down. Although the body will allow these levels to increase for a long time, at a certain point the top of the ladder will have been reached. And when that happens, we suddenly come crashing all the way down.

It's an effect similar to what happens when electrical wires overheat: they burn out. A person affected by burnout feels exhausted. For an extended period of time, any form of exertion, whether physical or mental, is too much. Recovery takes months, if not years. Things never quite return to the way they were.

Focus attention at the start rather than at the finish

Rather than always waiting until the last minute, when you feel the hot breath of time pressure breathing down your neck, it's far better to use the fresh spring breeze that's there at the start of an assignment to propel you forward.

As well as the physical effects we experience as we near the end of the allocated time for a project, something also happens on an energetic level the moment we get a new task or assignment – only this time it's much more positive. It feels as if the person who has given us the job is putting their trust in us or showing appreciation for work we've done in the past, and we immediately feel a certain excitement about the new challenge. It tingles and spurs us on. We also have an idea of what it will look like when it's done. We suddenly start getting ideas. If we give this energy free rein, more and more associations emerge. Various possibilities follow on each other's heels.

Here's an example of my own to illustrate this. I was asked to give a workshop on stress, working with employees on a boat that had been turned into a floating hotel. The company offered a combination of bike and boat travel to tourists from abroad.

What kind of stress would this job bring with it? Talking with the client provided the following information. Tourists and staff live side by side for ten days at a stretch. Some clients are demanding and want a different room or find the bike tours difficult. Their dietary wishes can also pose challenges to the kitchen. Prolonged periods of rain can have an effect on the moods of both guests and guides.

I hadn't had a group like this before and needed a lot more information.

What did I already know? What I realized immediately was this: it's about communication. It's about listening to requests and complaints and knowing how to respond to them, and it's also about knowing how to deal with someone who's in a bad mood.

What didn't I know? The boat is a confined area. How do people who barely know each other react under such circumstances? Do people have some degree of privacy? Is there somewhere they can go if they want to be on their own? How is it for the participant who finds they've overestimated their abilities and can't keep up with the active programme? I also really wanted to hear directly from a participant about such things as rest stops, preparations and when someone's patience is put to the test.

In summary, I asked myself the following questions: What do I know and what do I not know? What information do I need and how do I get it? Can I do it on my own or do I need someone to help me with the role-playing exercises I have in mind?

And what am I apprehensive about? Am I afraid of something? The questions are the same as for a gnawing rat. A gnawing rat, then, is no different from an assignment that hasn't been sufficiently explored.

When you take the time to do this at the start, it gets the motor running. The very next day I had a conversation with an acquaintance who I was surprised to learn had also worked as a guide on bicycle tours. You could call this a coincidence, but because I was open to the various aspects of the assignment, I had already started to talk about it at this stage, and this opportunity didn't go unnoticed. She told me about getting lost, about biking in the rain and flat tyres, and about participants who think they know more than the guide. This already gave me a better picture.

Then I spotted an article in the newspaper about a mining disaster in Chile. I read about the tensions that arise when people are forced to live together in an enclosed space for an extended period of time.

Before the end of the week, the plan inside my head was nearly finished and I wrote down the main points.

By using your imagination and making associations at the very start of an assignment, task or artistic endeavour, you open things up to your "inner instrument". This alerts you to useful information or assistance without having to suffer the unpleasant side effects of stress. You notice "coincidences" when you just happen to come across something that can contribute to the assignment.

What's more, you're now enthusiastic and talk about the project with the people around you. This also produces helpful responses, offers to collaborate or good advice. It goes from being a fearful story about something in the future to being an enjoyable project that inspires and excites you.

Instead of letting the bigger projects wait until they become urgent, you befriend them from the very start. In this way you allow your creativity to be engaged and to play with the project during the whole process.

EMAIL

Dealing with emails can be such a source of tension that we have created a special term for it: "email fatigue". In fact, suffering from email fatigue is so common nowadays that there are companies that focus exclusively on teaching people how to manage their inboxes and email habits more effectively.

Technological progress has meant that many aspects of our work and home life are more convenient, generally because we can do things faster. Unfortunately, the speed with which things happen actually produces more stress, so there is also a downside to those handy emails that make communication so much easier than when we used to write letters.

But what is it about emails specifically that causes this stress? The following aspects stand out:

- There are lots of them.
- They come in all day long, whether you like it or not.
- The sender expects you to respond quickly.
- Because there are so many, chaos can quickly ensue. Where do you put them all?

My inbox used to be filled to overflowing, and I would try to create order by marking important emails as unread. I could recognize these messages by the bold-faced type – but there were more and more of these as well.

When I opened Outlook, the program would give the number of unread emails. There would be hundreds of them. Every so often, I would delete the oldest ones from the inbox. This feeble attempt at managing my emails didn't exactly have a calming effect. There's a better and also easier way to do this. What you need most is insight into a number of the characteristics of your email traffic. And you can apply the principles of Time Surfing here as well.

What follows is a guide to preventing email fatigue.

Decide for yourself

To start with, decide for yourself when to open your email program. Adjust your settings to make sure your inbox doesn't open automatically as soon as you turn on your computer. Disable the pop-ups in the settings of your email program.

Let your intuition choose the time – not because it's going to know when an important message comes in, but because it weighs up all of your different activities energetically, and then picks a good moment. Of course there's also an element of curiosity, especially when you've just set something in motion and can expect to see a response to this by email. But it feels so much more powerful – and also much nicer – when you're in charge.

Be aware that, when dealing with your inbox, not all emails are equal. Just like reading different parts of the paper, you can spend varying amounts of time on each. You can spend an hour, half an hour or a few minutes on ten emails, or you can become absorbed in non-essential information. This depends on how much time you have available and on your mood.

Four options

The following are the four main courses of action when it comes to dealing with your email:

1. Reply
2. Delete
3. Allow to ripen
4. File

For every email, you determine which of these options is the right one.

1. Reply

Reply to those emails you don't have to give much thought to, such as answering a question or making an appointment or request. Try to keep your answers short and to the point. If it's going to take more time, it might be better to use the phone.

Sometimes you'll decide to do this right away, whenever you open your email program. At other times, you'll mark these kinds of emails and deal with them later on, one after the other, when your intuition chooses to do so. You'll go for this option when you don't want to be diverted from your main activity for too long.

2. Delete

Learn to throw emails away easily. Unsubscribe from newsletters you don't read. Make deleting emails into a regular activity. At the end of the day, have another look at the emails that came in that day and set the bar high for the ones you allow to stay in your inbox and also for those you are going to "allow to ripen". Also look at the rest of the emails you've saved over the past few days and delete what you can. It's important to make a habit of this last one, so that your inbox isn't cluttered with outdated emails. Enjoy how good and also how liberating it can feel to delete messages. The effect of having large numbers of emails without knowing what they contain is the same as for piles of unopened letters: it makes you feel agitated.

An inbox that's nearly empty feels just as good as an empty desk, and just as orderly.

3. Allow to ripen

Ripening, or simmering, is the method to use for an email you can't answer immediately. Examples of such emails are those messages you need to give more thought to, or which carry an emotional charge. By giving them a little time, it will be easier to find the right answer or the right tone.

These kinds of emails can stay in the inbox. You deal with them in a way that's similar to the one for gnawing rats. You let them sink in. Then time does the rest. After a while you'll suddenly know what you want to say or do, and you'll send a reply. So, your inbox doesn't have to be completely empty. It's almost empty. The messages that remain are the ones you want to answer a little later or those you want to allow to ripen before answering. Try to keep this group as small as possible, and give them a label, such as a flag or a star, depending on your email program.

4. File

When it comes to your emails, the most useful way to deal with them is to create a system of handy folders for storing your messages. The messages you want to save are filed according to category, which makes it easy for you to find a particular message later on.

I'll now set out a basic filing system, which you can use as a template. Take the time to make this system your own. It doesn't have to be perfect straight off the bat. Over time, you'll modify the names of the different folders and subfolders to better reflect what they contain and to meet your own needs.

Start by creating several main folders and number them. Your email program will automatically sort the folders according to number.

For example:

1. Your place of work or company.
2. A folder with your own name. This will be the folder for family and personal matters.
3. Organization or association you belong to.

Create subfolders in each main folder, and number these as well. If you create subfolders within a folder, you can start over and number them 1, 2, 3, and so on.

For a person who is self-employed, the main folder might look something like this:

1.1 Clients
    1. Companies
    2. Individuals
1.2 Suppliers
1.3 Marketing and publicity
1.4 Website
1.5 Workspace rental
1.6 Professional information

In the main folder that bears your name, your family and your friends each get their own subfolder.

2.1 Own family
    1. Name of your partner
    2. Name of your first child
    3. Name of your second child, and so on
2.2 Parents, brothers and sisters
2.3 Friends

Suggestions for other useful subfolders inside this main folder:

2.4   Orders
2.5   Subscriptions
2.6   Flight or train bookings

In the main folder "Volleyball club" (for which you're the treasurer), you can create subfolders such as the following:

3.1   Rental and maintenance
3.2   Finances
3.3   Events
    1. Open day
    2. Spring tournament
3.4   Newsletter
3.5   Minutes

Finally, make another subfolder in your inbox with the title "Nice to read or watch". In this folder, file those emails with links to videos, documentaries and articles that aren't urgent or essential but which you find interesting and would like to read or watch when you have a free moment. You don't have to immediately read in their entirety emails that contain more extensive, potentially useful, information. Have a brief look at these kinds of substantive emails so that you're aware of what information they contain, then file them in the appropriate folder.

Don't hesitate to create additional folders whenever that seems useful.

Transition

Now move the emails you want to save and be able to find again to the right folders. Working in this way makes it easier to deal with your email.

If you'd like to start using this system but still have 300 messages in your inbox, first move all of them to a separate, temporary folder.

Your inbox is now empty! Now create the folders and follow the instructions above. You can look in the temporary folder for the emails you need to refer back to and, after a number of months, you can delete whatever is left in this folder all at once.

Train yourself

Train yourself to keep moving and not to spend too much time on things. Reply, delete, allow to ripen or file. When you do this at the right moment, as you will once you've mastered Time Surfing – you'll also be able to do this effectively.

Be firm when it comes to emails that need to ripen. The only emails that should be given a place here are those you're going to answer in the near future but want to let sink in a bit first. All other emails should be deleted or filed, if necessary, in a new subfolder with a clear heading. Should you deem this necessary, you can occasionally give your mailboxes a thorough cleaning. You then delete old subfolders you no longer need, such as the one for last year's volleyball tournament.

Finally, should your inbox become cluttered again over time, create another temporary folder and repeat the instructions above. This time it will stick.

THE SMARTPHONE

My first cellphone was large and heavy, and had a stubby antenna sticking out of the top. I had a temporary job that required me to be on call, and I was provided with what was at the time a state-of-the-art piece of equipment. It was some years before I bought a cellphone of my own. I already had an appreciation for design and decided on a compact, impact-resistant sport model with rubber keys.

My next model was a flip phone. I had this one for years and, despite the tendency of the era, refused to get a new one. To start with, this was because it was an ethical issue for me. There was nothing technically wrong with my phone and I found it hard to replace something that still worked just fine. But my resistance was also due to the fact that I had seen at first-hand what the future had in store for me if I were to succumb ...

You see, my wife owned a smartphone. I saw the effect it had on her, and although I knew it was the "new normal", and although I knew that one day I too would probably own one, as far as I was concerned there was no need for that to happen as long as my small, easy-to-use model still worked.

When my wife turned 40, the children and I made a short film for the party – a slightly exaggerated send-up to the way she used her iPhone. First thing in the morning, a hand reached out from the bed for this magical device with its irresistible appeal, and it kept turning up throughout the rest of the film: at the breakfast table, on the garden bench, in the bathroom ...

And now, as I write these words, I've got my own smartphone right here beside me – and I'll readily admit I'd find it hard to get along without it.

In August, my family and I go to the Zen summer camp. The temple is located on the top of a mountain, at an elevation of 800 metres and, believe it or not, there is no reception there as of yet. We go through withdrawal during the first few days (for my son, this lasts for the first few weeks). Our sense of time gradually changes. We enjoy moments of doing nothing while we wait for the meal bell to sound. We sit in front of the tent with a book. We marvel at the dragonflies as they skim the surface of the stream, and admire their beautiful colouring. We unwind.

The smartphone tugs at us. It fills in the gaps. An empty moment becomes a social media moment. It can be filled by a snippet of news, adapted to the fleeting nature of the medium and presented as ever-shorter one-liners. We wonder if our Wordfeud opponent has answered yet. And how many likes the photo we just uploaded to Instagram has received. Maybe some new emails have come in. That bulky computer from the not-so-distant past now fits into our pocket or purse, and emits light and sound.

As with any transformation, at first you're very aware of what you're giving up. After a while, it becomes so commonplace that it becomes harder to imagine how things used to be. Anyone who cherishes what has been lost is living in another time and is considered old-fashioned.

So what is it that we've sacrificed, now that I'm still able to compare? And does the smartphone have an impact on harmonious Time Surfing?

What are we losing?

We lose the small, empty moments. But is that actually so bad? Those dull moments when you could use a little distraction are now quality moments. Wordfeud and other games are fun. They also connect us to others. News is important. Social media is communication.

Time Surfers will see these empty moments as an opportunity to take a breather, and will also recall its definition: taking a breather means doing something that

127

doesn't require you to think. Because it's precisely during those moments when the brain is left in peace and doesn't have to do anything for a while that your subconscious can emerge into the space that's been created and offer its suggestions and conclusions.

If you fill an empty moment with something that still requires your brain to focus, such as reading an article or doing something on your smartphone, this kind of spontaneous communication with our subconscious can't happen.

Will our breathers be ousted by the smartphone? The need to interact with your smartphone is a separate item, a separate bead. It is an intrusive bead – a temptation that we find difficult to resist, one that we involuntarily choose for our little in-between moments. As Time Surfers we will then also make the time for a breather when our bodies ask for it or when we finish a task. That's when our intuitive radar starts to turn and lets us know which task's time has arrived.

We also lose some of the face-to-face contact we have with people, and get remote exchanges in return. The reason for this is the possibility for video calls and the growing importance of social media. The smartphone does make this social media very accessible. However, the smartphone does make this social media very accessible. You can look at what people posted on Instagram while waiting for the bus or even while biking home, something you see some people doing. As for myself, I'm also glad to have found so many old friends again and I enjoy seeing how the family of my brother in Germany is doing. Also, the information usually contains visuals and the responses are often funny.

The price we pay for having such a wide array of contacts is that there's less direct contact. We don't have as much time for them as we used to and we also need them a little less.

However, there's also something amiss just below the surface. Even when we're with other people, we usually still make plenty of room for our remote relationships. In restaurants, you sometimes see everyone at a table checking their smartphones at the same time. At home, you might need to take a joint decision to turn off all phones and laptops at the end of the evening so that you can communicate directly for a while.

It takes time for a conversation to develop and become interesting or meaningful. I like to have participants on my communication courses experience the importance of small talk. At the start of a conversation, you talk for a bit about the weather, the trip or that nice new blouse. By doing so, we allow ourselves to get started and to get used to the other person. After a few minutes of small talk, we can go deeper.

The same applies to conversations at the family dinner table or with friends. When I was growing up and my family would sit together in the evening, I remember how it was only as the evening progressed that things would really get under way. The mood would become warm and intimate, and you wouldn't want to say goodnight. It's good to make time for the slower moving and more mundane preliminaries, because this creates an atmosphere where depth and connection can thrive.

You can't stand in the way of progress, and in any case we humans are better than any other animal at adapting swiftly to new circumstances. The same will also be true for our social behaviour. Our real needs will propel us to find new forms, and because of the tremendous creative capacities we humans possess, these new forms can only enrich us. As time goes on, I suspect that face-to- face exchanges will increasingly become something we have to consciously choose. We will come to see it as something special – something we will want to make time for because it has such a special quality. We will then have to bear in mind that this quality cannot be created instantaneously and needs time.

Practical tips for using smartphones

- When you want to do something on your smartphone, start and also finish what you're doing consciously (Instructions 1 and 2).
- While using a smartphone can be relaxing, it doesn't take the place of a breather. It serves as a distraction but still requires you to focus!
- Pay attention to the energy levels of both your body and your mind. When your attention flags, get up and take a breather (Instruction 3).
- Make time for personal contact. It's the most meaningful form of communication. During conversations, allow time for small talk and don't use social media.
- Mute your smartphone when your attention is required and enjoy the peace and quiet. It can be good to wait until after breakfast to turn on your smartphone. This gives you the opportunity to have a quiet start to your morning and to turn your focus inward at this important time of the day.

- Try to make your phone less attractive. Turn off all notifications except those you really need. Turn on focus mode or search in the settings under digital well-being and adjust the settings. Make sure you choose the phone, not the phone chooses you.

THE APPOINTMENT CALENDAR, WORKPLACE AND LISTS

The appointment calendar

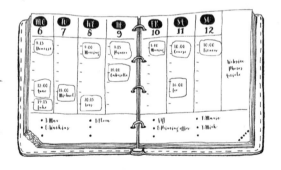

In your appointment calendar, you record appointments and delivery agreements. For the latter, you note down when something has to be finished. Also, jot down the short tasks you need to do on a particular day, such as answer a question or make a phone call, in the space provided in the calendar for that day.

Our appointment calendar provides us not only with an overview of our appointments, but also the opportunity to distribute them in a way that feels harmonious and spacious, and to make sure there is enough room between two appointments.

To be able to serve us well, our intuition needs to have accurate information about all of our time commitments so it is aware of the time it still has at its disposal. The more clearly the various time commitments are noted down, the better. Making use of different colours can be helpful here.

It's also important to record delivery agreements and highlight them in a particular colour. For reasons I've already explained, I prefer not to use the term "deadline" here because of the unpleasant association the term carries.

When you've agreed to have an assignment done in two weeks, or when you're going to give a training session on a certain date and you need to prepare for it beforehand, highlight this in your appointment calendar. Each clearly highlighted entry acts as an anchorage for the intuition, and allows it to navigate properly.

It works best if you look regularly at these fixed commitments, which you've reinforced with visuals. Also consult your schedule for the coming week, the following week and, in broad lines, your schedule for the coming month. This will give you both a short- and a long-term overview. The more information your intuition has at its disposal, the better it can perform.

Hidden delivery agreements

When you're organizing an event that will take place in a number of weeks, such as a talk, an opening or a party, the mailing for this has to be sent earlier. It's also handy to note down in your appointment calendar when this needs to happen.

If your calendar fills up entirely with appointments, plan in some unscheduled time. A good rule of thumb for this is between one and one and a half days a week.

Workplace

See to it that your workplace has a pleasing, uncluttered feel to it. Some people tend to leave the things they still need to do out in the open so that they don't forget to do them. A pile of letters here, a magazine article there. Colourful Post-its® containing telephone numbers stuck to the sides of the computer screen. At a neighbour's, I saw no fewer than eight different stacks of papers lined up shoulder to shoulder on the floor. As a result, she was constantly worrying about everything she still had to do instead of trusting she would be able to deal with everything at the right moment.

To give your desk this calm, clean quality, it's best to start by taking everything off it. Then wipe it down and arrange the things that are essential to you – monitor, keyboard and writing material – conveniently on the desk. Add something that you find beautiful or pleasing. A plant has a calming effect.

Your desk is now just like your head after you've examined and befriended everything: empty and available. As for the things that don't need to be on the desk, its best to sort them out and put them away. But if you don't have the time or energy for this immediately, you can place a small table next to your desk and put these things there temporarily. Later on, you can go through the various piles one by one: throw away what you don't need, sort out what you can file and finish what you can finish.

Start and end the day with an empty desk. Don't make your desk or workplace into a hidden agenda.

Lists

So, are lists really a thing of the past?

It's still good to use a list for what it is intended: realizing what you want to do in the future. A to-do list causes stress because it is a must-do list. Time and again you see what you have not yet done.

I suggest making a wish list in the morning. Before you even open your emails, write down everything you want to do today on a piece of paper. These are wishes, not demands. You don't rely on it. For each item you write down, also imagine what you will need to do to accomplish it. Then, turn the list over and take a breather! In this breather you choose your first task. In this way you can challenge yourself to navigate intuitively more and more, without using any force.

You can check every now and then to make sure you haven't forgotten anything, but gradually you will notice that you need it less and less. Make a new wish list every day and throw away the old one.

A checklist for trips

There is an occasion when having a list to hand is helpful, and that's when travelling. You don't have to keep reinventing the wheel about what you need to take on a trip, getting stressed as you try to remember everything.

You can make a list of everything, from your swimsuit to sunglasses, first-aid kit to flashlight. Such practical support can be reassuring right before departure, when most people end up getting nervous anyway.

Having an overview

In the same way that you make a list to reassure yourself, you can also occasionally make an overview. You write down your different tasks, along with their various components and connections. But once you've done this, you let it go again. As long as you can still see all the things you could possibly do, you'll get stressed. Your mind interprets this not as "this is going to happen" but as "this still has to happen". It sees a forceful current rather than a meandering stream.

You go ahead and create an overview because it provides you with additional support. It allows you to see what your rational mind wasn't aware of but which your intuition has known for some time. Now that you are aware of it, you can return to trusting.

THE "ICING ON THE CAKE"

Open your senses

As a Time Surfer, you experience every bead of the time-string more intensely. You embrace whatever it is you're doing, and carry out even those menial tasks such as ironing or chopping vegetables willingly and with care and attention.

The more you dare to trust your intuition – the more you let go – the more deeply you'll experience what you're doing, and the greater the sense of freedom you'll enjoy. You'll be less fixated on the result you want to achieve and find more satisfaction in the task itself.

Leading on from this, there are also what are known as "timeless" moments. In the film *Eat Pray Love*, an Italian explains the concept of *dolce far niente* – "the sweetness of doing nothing" – to Liz, an American. "We are masters of it!" he proclaims. So are the French. It's possible that the pleasant climate and being able to spend so much time out of doors invites this freedom to embrace "doing nothing" as a cherished activity.

Sometimes I invite myself to experience this "sweetness of doing nothing". I'll go and sit behind our house in the evening, where there's a big blue chest that serves as a bench in addition to providing storage. I sit down on it and do nothing – with no newspaper, no music, no email or Facebook to accompany me – simply nothing. In this way I create a piece of vacant time. After a while, all kinds of things are happening. Large mosquitoes flit beneath the mock-orange. Swifts soar overhead in ever-changing formations, shrieking with delight. Our local pigeon, which my wife has named Grugru, cautiously inches forward to inspect the cats' food bowls. She was born in the spring in a nest on top of the cupboard on our upstairs neighbour's balcony. The poplars around the tall silver buildings move gently in the wind.

When you do nothing, all kinds of things happen. When you don't fill in the blanks, anything is possible.

Timeless moments also arise when you lose yourself in what you're doing.

For me this happens when I make an origami bird with my son, dance at a party or go swimming with the children from the wooden pier in the canal not far from where we live. We play and we feel. And we literally forget the time. "Oh no, is it six o'clock already? Come on, we have to get home." A good book can have the same effect: you're intensely present as the story comes to life inside your head.

Let go of the reins

There are a great many moments that invite you to feel them. You can either accept or decline these invitations. But, before this can happen, you have to notice the invitation that's been extended to you.

Can you hear the rain tapping at the windows? Can you see the trees swaying gently in the wind? Can you feel the sun on your skin? Such moments can become more accessible to you with practice. To do this, you have to be willing to forgo the idea that everything has to serve some kind of purpose. You will gradually switch from goal-oriented behaviour to letting yourself be carried along by whatever happens. You let go of the horse's reins and let it choose the direction of travel. What happens next is open.

When you let go of control, you find a hidden treasure. Moreover, this treasure trove is boundless, because the possibilities are everywhere and all around us, there for the taking.

As a Time Surfer, you've already started to change course and move in this direction. And occasionally allowing yourself to experience what it's like to just float along with whatever happens is the icing on the cake.

Every time you experience a strong sensory stimulus, your senses send out an invitation. When you eat a dish that's new to you or one that's been prepared with a great deal of care, you naturally respond to this.

A passion fruit, with its seeds and soft, jelly-like interior, transports you to its tropical home.

Cockles have a unique flavour, strong and pungent – unlike anything else. My mother would sometimes fix them for us when we were growing up, first boiling them and then frying them in butter. Even as a child I ate them slowly, one at a time, because they were so special.

But you really don't need to wait for such a powerful invitation. Any kind of food can hint at this.

The best way to taste things with your senses is to slow things down a bit. Let a sip of juice slosh slowly around the inside of your mouth. Chew your food carefully. Let the flesh of soft fruits melt on your tongue.

You can do the same thing with your other senses, such as your sense of touch. It's a pleasant sensation to walk barefoot on grass or along the beach, through the water and over the warm sand.

When conditions permit and there's a gentle surf, I'll slip into the sea. I exhale completely so that my body is heavier than the water, and let myself sink to the bottom. Then I allow my relaxed body to be carried along by the swell of the waves as they rise and fall for as long as my breath will allow.

When you go camping and have a campfire, you feel the pleasant warmth on your skin. Certain kinds of wood are very aromatic, and the whole experience is a feast for the senses.

Of course, you can also respond to sensory stimuli at home. During a shower or bath, you can immerse yourself completely in how this feels. You can give your skin a massage while drying off.

This all seems so obvious, but often we're so much in our own heads that we forget to notice our sensory perceptions.

A strong stimulus might jolt our taste buds awake, only to be immediately overruled by our thoughts: What's in this? Isn't that cilantro? Mmm, nice. And that's about as far as it goes.

We can't stop our thoughts, but we also don't have to give them special attention when they're less than helpful. After observing that the person who did the cooking used cilantro, you can return to the senses and focus on what you're tasting.

The mild sensory stimuli that quietly beckon to us from the back of the room provide no immediate benefit and don't help us get ahead, but are more than worthy of our attention. They are the poetry of life!

Exercise

Every day, choose a few moments during which you will focus exclusively on what you touch, taste or notice. Some good opportunities for this:

- *shaving, combing your hair, skin care*
- *showering and lathering up*
- *drying off after a shower or bath*
- *tasting a dish*
- *washing the dishes and cleaning*
- *tasting pure juice or good wine*
- *looking at the clouds thoughts will arise in the meantime, and this is fine. Again and again, you invite yourself to feel. Be patient with yourself. Practice leads to mastery. When you're starting out, don't set the bar too high. The longer you do this, the more natural it will become.*

RETURNING TO WHAT COMES NATURALLY

Time Surfing is doing what comes naturally. When there's nothing urgent we have to do, when there's no pressure or obligation involved, this is our natural approach to time. We do it on Saturday afternoons and during vacations, at least if we can allow ourselves to let go and not be led by our self-imposed demands.

Returning to what comes naturally requires attention, and especially patience. But over the course of time, something remarkable happens. It keeps getting easier.

It's as if what comes naturally exerts a gentle pull and, like gravity, the closer you get, the stronger it becomes.

Therefore, think of this return to doing what comes naturally as a game, as an enjoyable voyage of discovery. The further you get and the more you can trust, the better things will be.

After a while, it will feel natural to give drop-ins your undivided attention. You'll know when you need to take a breather and you'll know that it feels good to work this way. Your system will get used to looking straight at those tasks and assignments that carry a negative charge, and will immediately want to befriend these potential gnawing rats.

Over time your actions will arise from a place of calm, in the same way that the waves on the ocean arise from the calm beneath the surface.

You'll find satisfaction in your work, and also in the things around you. You'll enjoy alternating between strenuous and relaxing tasks. And you'll often stop to notice small miracles as they pass: a cat wearing an amazed expression as it follows the flight of a butterfly, the perfume of honeysuckle wafting through the garden in the evening, the song of a blackbird perched on the rooftop or the wondrous look on the face of the little girl next door.

These are the golden beads that slip in and take their place among all of the other beads of the day. More and more you'll notice that they're all around you, everywhere you look, and are yours for the taking.

You can find more information about the work of Paul Loomans at timesurfing.uk or (in Dutch) at www.destressontknoping.nl and www.ikhebdetijd.nl.

ACKNOWLEDGEMENTS

I am grateful to:

Sonja, my wife ... for making it possible for me to spend so much time working on my book. Although I never actually rented that cottage in the country, I did end up spending a lot of time on my laptop in the midst of our lively family.

Master Myoken Bec ... from the very start and all along the way, you continued to encourage me to write this book and share my method.

Master Kosen Thibaut ... for showing me I could investigate everything for myself, even those faraway places everyone says you shouldn't go.

Brother Pieter and friend Pierre (Master Soko Leroux) ... for making me jealous of the way you relate to time, which showed me it's possible to live from a place of calm.

Olivier Provily ... for critically reading the manuscript and suggesting the original Dutch title.

Aielle Erens ... for your friendship and support.

Suzanne Paskamp ... for all of your advice and encouragement.

Niels de Hoog ... for believing in the book and for your wonderful illustrations.

Coleen Higgins ... for her sensitive translation.

Quirine Reijman ... for your immediate, intuitive "yes" to this project and for your dedication.

Daughter Dolly ... for your down-to-earth comments on the text I asked you to read.

Publishers Ankhhermes and Watkins ... for their confidence and flexibility, and also for the warmth in our working relationships.

Translator's acknowledgement

I would like to express my grateful thanks to my faithful sounding boards Maarten Groot and Mary Siegel, and also Sarah Deats and Jolyn Thompson.

**Follow the QR code for some good
advice from the author to put
Time Surfing into practice**